Railways of Looe and Caradon

by

J. M. Tolson : G. F. Roose

C. F. D. Whetmath

Published by:

FORGE BOOKS

42 Rectory Lane, Bracknell, Berks.

© 1974

The staff of the L. & C. and L. & L. railways at Moorswater in 1909. Fourth from left in the front row is H. Hawes, Stationmaster Looe, and to the right Septimus Bolton, Locomotive Superintendent, H. H. Holbrook, Superintendent of the Line, Inspector Scantlebury, Permanent Way Inspector, and A. Burridge, Stationmaster Liskeard.

PREFACE

The writing of this brief history of the Liskeard & Caradon and Liskeard & Looe Railways has brought together three people previously unknown to one another but the subsequent research and reconciliation of their often divergent views has afforded much pleasure. The history of a railway unconnected to the main railway system of the country for over fifty years yet able to exist profitably because of its association with the all too brief heyday of the Cornish mining industry in the middle of the nineteenth century has proved an interesting study. Now the mines of Caradon lie in ruins and the railway serving them has been removed for over fifty years yet the attraction of these bleak moors occasioned a recent proposal for a narrow gauge steam railway on the trackbed of the upper section of the Liskeard & Caradon Railway. Nothing came of this but the current emphasis on the development of the country's own mineral resources may in time cause the bustle and sounds of the mining industry to echo once again across the now deserted slopes of Caradon.

ACKNOWLEDGEMENTS

Many people have assisted in the preparation of this brief account. In particular the authors wish to record their thanks to the Archivist, British Railways Board (now attached to the Public Record Office) for providing facilities for research; British Railways staff at Bristol and Plymouth; J. Chaston; Mrs E. F. E. Holbrook; A. R. Kingdom; Major Kitson; W. H. Paynter who has a museum at Looe housing several relics from the railway; C. J. Seccombe; A. F. Tucker; R. V. Walling; Cornish Times and Western Morning News. The manuscript was typed by Joan Tolson and the maps and plans drawn by F. J. Mackett. Kind permission to use photographs has been given by British Railways (p. 48); R. N. Joanes (p. 72); C. Lockhart (p. 41); Locomotive & General Railway Photographs (pp. 22, 29, 37, 38, 51 below, 53, 56, 62, 64, 65, 67, 68); R. Raddy (pp. 8, 18); Real Photographs (p. 54); R. J. Sellick (cover, p. 59); D. C. Vosper (p. 25); the remainder are from the authors' collections. Special mention must be made of the late W. E. Hayward's collection of photographs, tickets and other relics now in the hands of the Public Record Office.

Cover illustration shows No. 5572 at Looe with a train from Liskeard in 1959. This locomotive has been preserved by the Great Western Society.

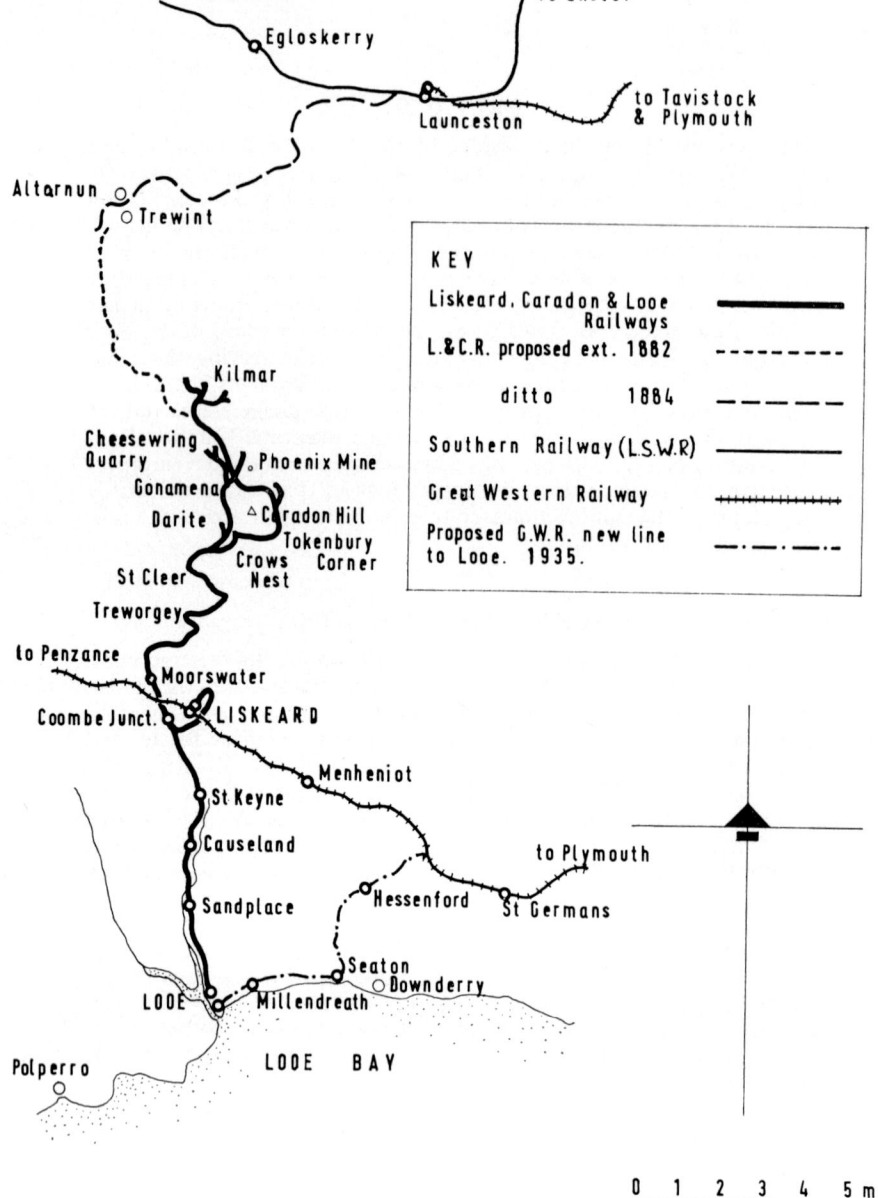

to Padstow   to Exeter

Egloskerry

to Tavistock
& Plymouth

Launceston

Altarnun
Trewint

KEY

Liskeard, Caradon & Looe
                  Railways

L.&C.R. proposed ext. 1882

ditto   1884

Southern Railway (L.S.W.R)

Great Western Railway

Proposed G.W.R. new line
to Looe. 1935.

Kilmar

Cheesewring
Quarry

Phoenix Mine

Gonamena
Darite

Caradon Hill
Tokenbury
Crows   Corner
Nest

St Cleer

Treworgey

to Penzance

Moorswater

Coombe Junct.

LISKEARD

Menheniot

St Keyne

Causeland

to Plymouth

Sandplace

Hessenford

St Germans

Seaton
Downderry

LOOE

Millendreath

Polperro

LOOE   BAY

0   1   2   3   4   5 m.

INTRODUCTION

The rugged southern coast of Cornwall with its many coves and harbours renowned in the past as the home of fishermen and smugglers, is now one of Britain's principal holiday areas while the hinterland, once a thriving mining area, offers its often somewhat desolate beauties to the tourists. The picturesque old-world town of Looe is known to us nowadays as a pleasant holiday resort of some 4,000 inhabitants which includes the exciting and rather exotic sport of shark fishing among its numerous attractions. Consisting of two separate townships, East and West Looe, built on opposite sides of a deep river valley, so steep-sided as to be almost a gorge, it is a port of considerable antiquity although its maritime commercial activity is now almost at a standstill. The river flowing through the narrow harbour neck to gain the sea is in fact two separate streams, the East and West Looe Rivers, which flow together just above the town, and at their confluence at high tide is formed the wide expanse of water or "loch" from which the town reputedly takes its name. In the upper reaches of the West Looe River was the celebrated Herodsfoot lead mine which after a prosperous career combined with an almost continual struggle against flooding, ceased large scale operations in 1884, although sporadic working continued until 1904. The East Looe River flows up a twisting valley to Moorswater and thus forms a natural link between the twin townships and the once important mining centre of Liskeard, now a quiet market town of some 5,000 inhabitants, but in the Middle Ages a "stannary" town to which the miners brought their metal to be weighed, assayed and taxed. Liskeard was also once the seat of the ancient princes of Cornwall and in 1240, Richard, the brother of King Henry III, granted it a Royal Charter as a free borough, although the Corporation in its more modern form dates only from 1586, and in 1885 the town was disfranchised as an independent borough. Moreover the Reform Act of 1832 had also ended its Parliamentary importance as since 1294 it had been empowered to send two Members to Westminster.

West Looe, as one of the seaports for the mines and the whole rich agricultural region around Liskeard, became a seigneural borough in 1243, but although East Looe had elected a Member of Parliament since the 14th century, its western neighbour did not enjoy this privilege until some 200 years later. As a busy medieval port, Looe possessed ships of its own both for peaceful trade and to be requisitioned by the King for the all too frequent wars of the period, and indeed in 1346 East Looe alone sent 20 ships and 315 men to assist Edward III at the siege of Calais, only 5 ships less than the city of London itself could muster at that date.

Gradually, however, despite the importance of its fish curing industry, Looe became overshadowed as a port by the development of Fowey and Plymouth but nevertheless West and East Looe became legally constituted boroughs in 1574 and 1588 respectively with their powers, responsibilities and duties clearly defined, and the Corporations lasted in this form until 1869 and 1886 but like Liskeard they too lost their right to elect Members of Parliament in 1832.

Out to sea off Hannafore Point is Looe Island (or St. George's Island) rising 149ft out of the sea and at almost one mile in circumference the largest island off the southern coast of Cornwall. In earlier days there was both a chapel and a gun battery on it and one of the legends in which this area abounds indicates that St. Joseph of Arimathea was a tin merchant and landed there bringing the Child Jesus with him. Tin was almost certainly mined in the area in the Bronze Age as it was needed to mix with copper to form bronze and being near the surface or in streams was not difficult to find. Cornwall may very well have been the Cassiterides of the Phoenician merchants, the Western isles to which they came for tin where at a place called Ictis, variously reputed to have been the Isle of Wight or St. Michael's Mount, they loaded the cargoes of metal.

Whatever legends may say, there is no doubt that by the 11th century tin mining at least had become a veritable industry and although ore was still to be found by "streaming", this method was providing diminishing returns and the miners followed the lodes which outcropped on the hills to form primitive open cast mines, which consisted of huge trenches known as "rakes" whose relics are still to be seen on the hills of Devon and Cornwall. In later years this method too became unproductive and small mine shafts with underground galleries proliferated in the 18th and 19th centuries to usher in the canal and railway age. This was to provide new life for the port of Looe whose small but varied and prosperous trade, particularly in pilchards, had been almost killed by the blockades of the Napoleonic Wars. Much of the new prosperity was occasioned by the opening of a canal between Moorswater and Looe although it was not primarily built for mineral traffic but rather for the transhipment of agricultural produce and fertiliser. But soon a whole new industry was to spring up in the hinterland near Caradon and the Cheesewring and bring with it a specialised and romantic vocabulary in which "captains, adventurers and tributers" came to work the "setts" using "crushers", "whims", and wheels operating "twelve heads of stamps".

CHAPTER 1

The Liskeard & Looe Union Canal, and the Growth of the Caradon Copper Mines

The idea of an artificial waterway linking Liskeard and Looe had been discussed as early as 1777, when certain inhabitants of the latter town, their interest aroused by the building of the St. Columb Canal and the authorisation of the Bude Canal, asked the eminent canal engineer, Edward Leach, to survey a route for a waterway for transporting sand and lime, then much in demand as fertilisers, between Looe and the inland farms. This was to take the form of a canal running from Bank Mill Bridge, 2½ miles from Liskeard, to Sandplace, 2 miles above East Looe, involving a cut no less than 15 miles long against a mere eight by river and containing two inclined planes. Its estimated cost was £17,500 and a yearly income of £2,500 was expected, while the possibility of a further extension to St. Germans to facilitate trade with Plymouth was also discussed. The project lapsed as did further schemes at the turn of the century for the cost was far too high for the relatively limited resources of the people involved.

It was not until August 1823 that events took a more positive turn when a public meeting was held in Looe to discuss the possibilities of a turnpike road, canal or railroad to link Liskeard and Looe. James Green, a well-known canal engineer, was charged with surveying these alternative means of transport, and produced plans in less than a fortnight, probably by using the levels from previous canal surveys. He too felt that the descent of the valley would be too steep for normal locks, the supply of water being a constant problem, so he recommended the use of inclined planes suitable to carry 4 ton boats to overcome the difference in levels at critical points.

The basic scheme consisted of two canals, a channel 28ft wide and 4ft deep, from Tarras Pill past Sandplace to Causeland, with a lock so that the limestone barges could reach Sandplace, where lime kilns were to be set up. Above Causeland would be a smaller canal 19ft wide at the top and 3ft deep over which the 4 ton boats could be hauled in trains of ten and then taken over the two inclined planes. The estimated cost was £14,000 and, as in the 18th century scheme, it was designed to be a mainly agricultural canal, carrying fertilisers and coal upstream and farm produce to the sea, although tolls were fixed for the copper ores which were to provide much of its income in later years.

But, although the plans and sections drawn up by Green were deposited for the Parliamentary Bill in October 1823, the promoters were not altogether happy and asked three other people, John Edgcumbe, Robert Coad and Thomas Esterbrook, to carry out a

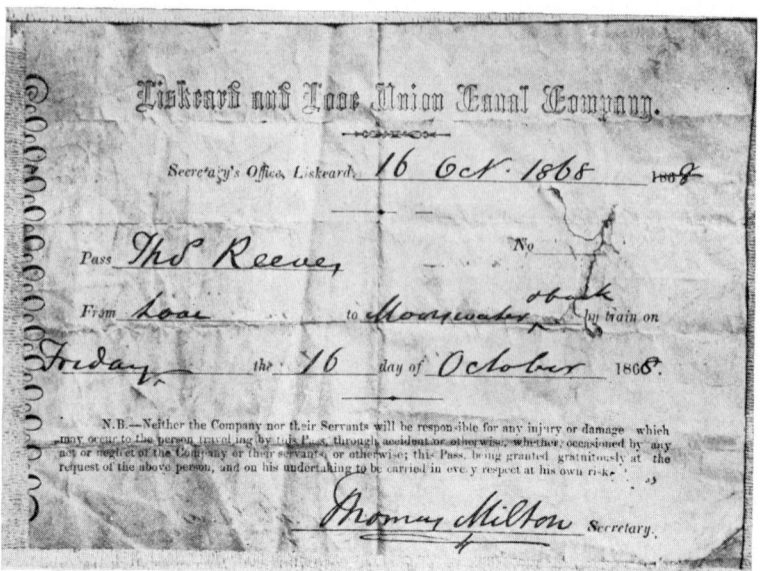

Railway Free Pass issued by the Canal Company

further survey. The first of these three was a Liskeard agricultural engineer who, when advertising his threshing machines, flour mills and cider presses, added seemingly as an afterthought "Canals cut on a new patent plan 18ft wide and three feet deep with all apparatus complete, in good ground, £900 per mile". His advert ended by recommending "Edgcombe's New Patent Inclined Plane". But, as we shall see, his ideas must have changed in the meantime for the joint survey provided for a 26ft canal 4ft deep, and without inclined planes, from the east side of the Looe River at Moorswater, 1½ miles from Liskeard, crossing the river near Trussel Bridge and running on the west side to Corgolan Bridge with a wider canal from there past Sandplace to Tarras Pill near Duloe. As its course involved a rise of no less than 156ft in 5 miles 7 furlongs, it contained 25 locks including a large river lock at the southern end. This scheme satisfied the majority of the interested parties and, although a few queried the wisdom of altering Green's plans at this late stage, the Bill for its construction had a relatively swift passage through Parliament and received the Royal Assent on June 22nd 1825. The Liskeard & Looe Union Canal, as the enterprise was called, was authorised to raise £13,000 capital in £25 shares with additional powers to obtain a further £10,000 by mortgage or loans if necessary, and within a very short time £10,500 had been raised from 134 shareholders. The Act empowered the Promoters to cut the canal, make several roads to communicate with the waterway and to take water from the East Looe River and the

Crylla Rivulet. They could also use part of the latter as a feeder provided that the navigation of the River Fowey, of which the Crylla was a tributary, was not affected and, to check on this, two Engineers were to be appointed, one by the company, and the other by the Mayor and Corporation of Lostwithiel. Sanction was also given for the use of rollers and inclined planes if necessary in place of locks, while the canal was to be 4ft deep, 14ft wide at the bottom and 26ft at the top. Robert Coad was appointed Engineer with Robert Retallick as Superintendent of Works and these two soon had the line of the canal laid out although they were not without their critics. Even at that busy time the Directors found time to think of the welfare of the canal navvies for at the Board Meeting on September 2nd 1825, it was resolved "that Mr Robert Rean of East Looe be Surgeon and Apothecary to attend the labourers working on this canal and that sixpence per month be deducted from the wages of each person employed, as a Remuneration to him for his services"—an early form of company health insurance scheme.

Five years had been allowed for its construction but this proved ample time as the canal was partially opened on August 27th 1827, and taken into use throughout its length in March of the following year.

The Lords of the Manor and other interested parties were allowed to build wharves and warehouses along the banks with prior permission of the Company. The original list of tolls makes interesting reading in view of the many items which appear strange to our modern eyes:

Tonnage and Wharfage Rates

	s. d.
	per ton per mile
For all limestone, culm or coal for burning, Lime, Sand, Oreweed, Dung or any other Manure, except Salt and Burnt Lime, Building Stone, Free-stone, Granite, Clay and Stone for making Roads	0. 3½.
For Lime	0. 7.
For all Wheat, Barley, Oats, Bran, Flour, Meal and Potatoes	0. 10.
For all Tin, Copper, Lead, Iron and all other Metals having been smelted, Bricks, Tiles, Timber, Charcoal, Deals, Wood, Faggots, Bark, Seeds, Vetches, Peas, Paper, Old Junk or Rags, Salt and all other Goods, Wares, Merchandise and Things whatever, Hay, Straw, Cattle, Calves, Sheep, Swine and Other Beasts	1. 1½.
For all Goods, Wares, Merchandise and Things landed on any Wharf, but not remaining more than seventy two hours	9./ton
For ditto, after the first seventy two hours per day	6./ton

Fractions of a ton to be taken as the Quarters therein, and of a Quarter as a Quarter
Fractions of a mile as the Quarters, and of a Quarter as a Quarter.

9

Authority to construct a plateway between Liskeard and Looe had also been contained in the Canal Act but this was allowed to lapse in favour of the Canal, although the Company did build a new road between Liskeard and Moorswater to avoid a steep hill on the existing route. The total cost of the Canal was £17,200 against the estimated £12,577 6s od but as this included the building of the road and other unforeseen expenses including £600 compensation paid to a local landowner, the costs were reasonably well contained and the Company managed to pay a 6% dividend in 1829, the first full year of working, and rarely failed to maintain 5% throughout its life. By 1838 it was justifiably said of the waterway "Liskeard has benefited beyond most other towns . . . by a canal from the port of Looe which affords a cheap and easy conveyance for lime, the most important of all manures in that district", although we must not forget that other composts, coal, stone and minerals were being transported more cheaply than ever before.

But the traffic of the Looe Canal was soon to be changed for as the mid-thirties brought a slump in the agricultural traffic of the area, so providentially the opening and fantastic growth of large copper and tin mines in the remote hilly moorland of the Caradon area, north of Liskeard, between 1837 and 1840, provided a new and far more lucrative trade. Although it was to be only a brief half century before all were closed, there were soon twenty five mines at work in the area where every available acre was taken up for mining purposes. Apart from a few small tin mines, there had been nothing of note in the area until in 1837 Captain James Clymo and his two sons, leading a team of miners, made the first strike which became the greatest of the mines, the South Caradon, founded for a mere £640 but paying annual dividends up to £10,000 in the 1840s. By 1844 410 people were employed there, many having come from the declining mines of Western Cornwall, and the mine, 90 fathoms deep, has been described as being equipped with a "30in pumping engine, a 26in crusher, a 22in whim plus a 31ft × 2ft water wheel for drawing ore and a 18ft × 2ft wheel operating twelve head of stamps".*

The second great mine, West Caradon, was founded shortly before 1840 and financed by Liskeard merchants and bankers; dividends came quickly, the mine being 70 fathoms deep and employing 250 people within 4 years, although the original outlay involved was £6,000, almost ten times the sum the Clymo adventurers had required to start South Caradon. Nevertheless by the early 1850s this mine was richer even than South Caradon and the deepest in the Caradon district. In 1850 over 550 people were employed there and improvements were continually being made with a 50in pumping engine replacing the original 30in engine soon afterwards, although the existence of the mine was seriously threatened by a mechanical breakdown which caused the water level to rise alarmingly.

*The Mines and Mineral Railways of East Cornwall and West Devon (D. B. Barton).

Despite these two successful ventures, there were many failures even though new setts were sunk into the rich Caradon lode at various points. Other mines in the area such as Craddock Moor, Caradon Consols, Wheal Norris and Gonamena Mines, were also far less successful and more intermittently worked although in their heyday some employed over 200 persons. Others such as East Caradon, Glasgow Caradon Consols, a later revival of the Tokenbury Mine started in 1841, and the Marke Valley Mines proved more profitable in later years and will be described more fully in a further section.

Tin had also been mined in the area since before the eighteenth century for there was a great mile long lode which had outcropped in the region to the east of the Cheesewring and even as early as 1730 a Newcomen steam engine was at work there. In 1836 the Cornwall Great United Mining Association with James Clymo as one of its captains began work in the area but disputes led to its failure although the immense sum of £50,000 had been spent in floating the scheme. In December 1842 operations recommenced and mining of both copper and tin led to a steady growth in output of the Phoenix United mines with over 150 people employed there. Profits were relatively modest although by 1860 almost £150,000 had been paid out in dividends, and the mine was 216 fathoms deep, producing some of the richest copper ores in Cornwall at that time. In the area around Liskeard too, mining had also found a new impetus. Here, however, the mineral was lead from two long lodes on either side of the town, the first being mined by the Herodsfoot Mine in the upper valley of the West Looe River, and the other, near Menheniot, some distance to the east. The most notable mine there was Wheal Mary Ann, whose principal adventurer was Captain Clymo, the discoverer of South Caradon, who was also involved in the other great lead mine of the Menheniot area—Wheal Trelawny.

Liskeard & Caradon Railway.
EXCURSION.
LOOE to MOORSWATER
AND BACK. (S1)
FIRST CLASS—Not Transferable.
Available only by Train for which issued,
and subject to Conditions published.

840

CHAPTER 2

Two Railways at Moorswater

With such rapid expansion of traffic between the Caradon area, Liskeard and Looe, the age-old problem of transport between the mines and the canal basin at Moorswater presented almost insuperable difficulties. Wagons and packhorses were used to carry the ever-increasing tonnage over almost non-existent roads which were frequently impassable in bad weather and it was estimated that the cost of carrying coal and ore in this way to and from Caradon was 4s 6d a ton—a most uneconomic proposition. On the other hand, the canal tolls on ore for the journey between Moorswater and Looe had been reduced to 1s 3d per ton in 1838 and still further to 1s 0d four years later while in 1843 the toll on coal was also reduced from 3s to 2s per ton. An alternative method of transport was quickly sought and as the original Liskeard & Looe Union Canal Act had contained authority to construct a plateway, the idea of building a railway from the Caradon mines to the Canal at Moorswater was mooted by the proprietors of the South and West Caradon Mines and some of the Canal Proprietors, and quickly found a wide support. Thus on July 27th 1843 the Liskeard & Caradon Railway was incorporated to construct a 4ft 8½in gauge line some 6¼ miles in length from the terminal basin of the canal at Lamellion Bridge, Moorswater, to South Caradon, with an extension of the main line to Tokenbury Corner and a branch to the Cheesewring which would link the tin and copper mines of the former and the granite quarries of the latter to the Canal and thus provide easy access to the port of Looe. Granite from these quarries was used for forts and docks at Plymouth, Spithead and Portsmouth, for the new Westminster Bridge and the breakwaters at Alderney, Dover and Portland. Much of it was dressed and polished at Looe before transhipment and some of this was used for the base of the Albert Memorial in London and in the construction of the Thames Embankment.

The L. & C. Act further empowered the company to raise capital of £12,000 in 480 shares of £25 each and up to £4,000 by loans or on mortgage. The promoters of the line had distinguished themselves by laying before Parliament a Bill containing no less than 344 clauses which led certain eminent people to consider that its construction should have been left to private enterprise without the need for a special enactment but, despite this, its supporters secured permission for their line to cross several turnpike roads on the level provided that horses were used instead of locomotive power, each contravention of this proviso to carry a fine of £50. Moreover the Act stipulated that

milestones were to be set up every quarter mile and no tolls could be levied until these and the toll boards with lists of tolls had been erected. The line was to rise through 650ft in about 6 miles on a ruling gradient of 1 in 60 with the intention of gravity working of loaded wagons in the seaward direction. These were to be sent down separately in the evening, each under the control of a brakesman. The empties could then be hauled back in the morning to the mines and quarries by horses owned by the company and stabled for the most part at Moorswater.

Construction was relatively speedily carried out as granite block sleepers were obtained from the Cheesewring Quarry and the rails carried free of charge by the Canal Company. A section of line 5 miles 60 chains in length running from Moorswater by a somewhat circuitous route through Tremabe, St. Cleers and Crows Nest to the mines at South Caradon was opened on November 28th 1844, while the 3 mile extension to the Cheesewring Quarry and Wheal Phoenix Mine came into operation in March 1846. This reached its destination by means of an inclined plane on a gradient of 1 in 11 at Gonamena on the west side of Caradon Hill while a short incline owned by the West Caradon Mine connected the higher part of the sett to the Cheesewring branch below the Gonamena incline. The cost of construction of the line had greatly exceeded the original authorised capital and the company was also in financial difficulties because some of the shares had been forfeited by their holders to avoid payment of the calls upon them. So the Canal Company took up 25 shares at a total cost of £625 and the mine owners purchased the rest—an act which substantially reduced their dividends. Nevertheless on June 25th 1847 the L. & C. was empowered to raise further capital of £10,500 and loans of up to £3,500. In due course a total of 861 shares was taken up but even those subscribers who had not forfeited their holding were slow to pay their calls and only £7,175 had been raised in this way while no loans had yet been forthcoming. As the total cost of the line had been £25,170 or £2,850 per mile, including £1,820 for the land, construction costs of £20,900 and £2,450 for the two Acts of Parliament, finance was bound to be the main preoccupation of the Directors, despite the extra capital authorised, as the tolls for ore and coal were fixed at the relatively modest sum of 4d per ton per mile.

The L. & C., even when opened throughout, was isolated from the rest of the railway system of the country and although the incorporation of the Cornwall Railway on August 3rd 1846 gave the local company hope that this isolation would soon be ended, it was in fact to last for another 55 years. The Cornwall Railway had been authorised to construct a line from Plymouth to Falmouth and to raise capital of £1,600,000 together with loans of up to £533,333. The Act also contained provision for the company to construct a connection to the Liskeard & Caradon Railway and to purchase or lease both that line and the canal to Looe. This provision had been made after the Canal company had made known its opposition to the original Cornwall Railway scheme for a branch to Looe which would have almost

certainly meant the end of the waterway. But this was the time of the "Railway Mania" and these aspirations proved too great for the company even though the project was supported by the Great Western, Bristol & Exeter and South Devon Railways. The abandonment of the connection to the L. & C. together with certain other schemes was sanctioned by Board of Trade Warrant in 1852 and the C.R. shareholders were so informed in April of that year. When the Cornwall Railway was formally opened for passenger traffic between Plymouth and Truro on Wednesday, May 4th 1859, it was to the 7ft 0¼in gauge and as it passed 150ft above the standard gauge L. & C. on the mighty Moorswater Viaduct, it was clear that no satisfactory outlet would come from that quarter in the foreseeable future.

During the construction of the Liskeard & Caradon line, it had been felt that the existing harbour facilities at Looe were insufficient to cope with the expected volume of traffic, and at a public meeting on February 5th 1845 these sentiments were forcibly voiced. It was decided the port should be improved in conjunction with the canal and in 1848 the Looe Harbour Commissioners were established, one of whom was to be the Treasurer of the Canal Company. With the increasing traffic from the copper mines after the completion of the L. & C. in 1846, the Canal was able to pay off its mortgage debt without affecting its 5% dividends and with an increasingly healthy bank balance. From a total of 24,000 tons in 1849, its traffic increased to 36,000 tons in 1854 while in the same year the L. & C. carried no less

Phoenix United mine showing track laid on stone blocks in the foreground

than 20,500 tons including 9,815 tons of copper ore, 3,364 tons of granite and a large quantity of coal for use at the mines and quarries.

It was announced at the Annual General Meeting of the Canal Proprietors that the profit from the traffic carried in 1854 amounted to £1,447 3s 8d and a dividend of 25s 0d "free of income tax" was declared. This was to remain a standard figure for many years to come even though a mere two years later the operating profit had risen to £2,142 15s 7d. This was a deliberate policy of the Committee of Management who concentrated on investing the surplus or using it to pay off loans as quickly as possible rather than merely pandering to the desires of the shareholders. This was all the more praiseworthy as the Committee, which at that time had such notables as Peter Clymo the Younger, Edward Geach, Thomas Sargent and Richard Retallick among its members, were not only shareholders but gave their services free so that the Minutes of each A.G.M. contained a rather quaint vote of thanks to the Committee "for the gratuitous services rendered by them during the past year". The wisdom of the Committee's policy, which also placed great emphasis on chasing up debtors at every opportunity, was amply demonstrated in the difficult times to come.

By the late fifties the Liskeard & Caradon Railway was carrying almost 40,000 tons of freight a year at the following basic tolls:

Ores, coals, bricks	4d per ton per mile
Lime, limestone, culm, manure, granite, slate	2d per ton per mile
Corn, potatoes, hay, cattle, salt and other goods	6d per ton per mile

As traffic from the mines grew, interchange facilities at Moorswater became more and more cramped and in the Canal Committee minutes for January 23rd 1856 it is recorded that more land was to be leased to the Gonamena and Craddock Moor Mines for use as ore yards and an additional rent of £2 per annum was to operate from March 25th. In that same year, 1856, the Canal carried no less than 48,000 tons of freight at a profit of £1,783. Nevertheless, the Committee of Management decided that capacity had been reached and drastic measures would be needed to cater not only for the ore and granite traffic but also for the increasingly important back cargo of coal to the mines and quarries. One suggestion was to extend the Canal nearer to Looe but the Committee, mindful of the provision for a plateway in the original Canal Act of 1825, decided on June 10th 1857 to ask two of the Canal Engineers, Messrs Jenkin and Trathan, to prepare an estimate for constructing a railway from Moorswater to Looe. As a result of this, the Proprietors were given a full statement of the problems and their possible solution. The capacity of the canal had been strained to the utmost by its existing traffic particularly at certain times of the year when the lack of an adequate water supply made passage through the many locks a very slow process. This had become such an obstacle that the L. & C. Railway had several times been forced to divert some of its traffic to Calstock. Moreover, at this time too, the Cheesewring Granite Company was proposing to build a plateway from its quarries to the L. & C. which would enable it to increase its output still further. It had also been found that it cost between 4d and 6d a ton to tranship goods between canal and railway at Moorswater, although in the early days the other savings were such that this was not considered important, now the Committee recommended to the Proprietors the building of a railway from Moorswater to Tarras Pill beside the canal, which was not proposed for abandonment at this stage, and then along the eastern shore of the estuary to Looe. It was to be financed by the Canal Company which, because of its sound financial position, could utilise the original borrowing powers of the 1825 Act to raise the capital. It was estimated that the line would cost about £11,000 exclusive of rolling stock and Parliamentary expenses, the relatively low cost being made possible as the Canal Company owned most of the land necessary for its construction.

This scheme was approved at a special General Meeting of the Proprietors on Tuesday, October 13th 1857, and ten days later at a meeting attended by Edward Geach the Looe Harbour Commissioners confirmed their agreement to provide terminal facilities and quays for the mineral traffic. A proposal for building a branch to West Looe was rejected by the Committee on November 4th 1857 as on the basis of the estimates submitted by Messrs Jenkin and Trathan, they felt the expense to be unjustified.

Work on formulating the Bill to lay before Parliament continued steadily and on January 6th 1858 the Committee gave instructions to apply to the Clerk of the Private Bill Office of the House of Commons for his warrant to deposit £900 at the Bank of England in the name of the Accountant General in compliance with the standing orders of Parliament. The draft of the Bill was approved at two special meetings of Proprietors on February 2nd and April 24th 1858, and on May 11th the Liskeard & Looe Railway Act received the Royal Assent. By this the Liskeard & Looe Union Canal Company obtained powers to construct a railway 7 miles 3 chains in length from an end-on junction with the Caradon line at Moorswater to Looe Bridge where access would also be provided to the quay to facilitate speedy transhipment of freight. Capital was to be £13,000 in £25 shares to be provided by the Canal Company who were also empowered to raise a further £4,000 on mortgage or bond. The Committee offered the 520 shares thus generated to each of the existing shareholders to the extent of their present holding, and even by the Special General Meeting of June 25th 1858 all had been taken up and no less than £6,660 9s 7d already subscribed. The final estimated cost of the railway, on which the steepest gradients were originally to be 1 in 63, was £12,000 and as some ten acres of land were required for additional works three years was allowed for its compulsory purchase and five years for the construction of the line. The company was also authorised to make working arrangements with the L. & C. which it ultimately did.

Silvanus W. Jenkin had been appointed Engineer with Mr Trathan to assist him and by the beginning of June he had obtained quotations for rails from various manufacturers as follows:

Plymouth Iron Co.	£7 os	od per ton
Ystalyfera Co.	£7 os	od per ton
Guest & Co.	£6 15s	od per ton
Rhymney Iron Co.	£6 6s	od per ton

As might be expected, the Committee opted for the cheapest as in an order of 500 tons a great deal of money could be saved. This was a busy time for these worthy gentlemen as the operation of the Canal had to be more closely supervised than ever now that saturation point had been reached. So it was not until October 16th 1858 that they finally instructed the Engineers to obtain tenders for the construction of the line from Moorswater to Tarras Pill either as a single lot or in four sections. Tenders for the building of bridges were to be submitted separately while it was hoped to get the Duchy of Cornwall to remit the tolls on the granite blocks required for sleepers to reduce costs still further. On November 15th the tender of £1,278 14s od for building the line submitted by John Brown and William Williams was accepted and eight days later the bridge contract was given to Messrs Firks, Bone and Sargent with the proviso that costs were under no circumstances to exceed £2,000. Early in the following year the construction of the Tarras Pill–Looe section was also put out to tender and after several ranging from £1,257 13s 6d to £1,564 6s od had been reviewed on May 30th 1859, the lowest of those submitted by Messrs Bone & Firks—without Mr Sargent this time—was accepted. Early in January 1860 the Engineers decided that the section of line through the Looe Estuary and Tregarland to Looe Quay should be laid on wooden sleepers instead of granite blocks. Despite every effort to keep costs down and the relatively healthy financial situation of the Canal Company, the construction estimates of the new line were proving overly optimistic and the Committee was forced to consider loans from various people. By February 1860 these amounted to £6,750 of which Peter Clymo had advanced £2,000 to which he was to add another £1,000 in the following May. Throughout the whole of 1860 the Committee concentrated much of its efforts on chasing debtors and shareholders who were tardy in paying the calls on their shares to time. On May 10th the Engineers were instructed to carry out only those works necessary for the completion and operation of the line but nevertheless by the time it was completed the costs had risen to £20,140. Finally, in spite of all their efforts the Committee had to obtain authority to borrow an additional £7,000 and this was granted to them on October 1st 1860. Moreover in order to operate the line at minimum cost, it had been agreed that the Canal Company

Looe: (*above*) *a view taken prior to construction of the passenger station and* (*below*) *an early view of the passenger station.*

should purchase or hire a steam locomotive while the Liskeard & Caradon Railway would supply the trucks. These arrangements will be discussed in detail in Chapter Six.

Naturally the Committee were anxious that the railway should be opened for traffic as soon as possible and on December 13th 1860 it was resolved to open the line on December 27th. Although like the Liskeard & Caradon Railway, at this date the line was intended purely for the transport of freight and minerals, this was not allowed to prevent the locals from having a ceremonial opening and the Engineers were instructed to fix up wagons to enable the Committee and those of the Proprietors and the general public who were interested, to have a ride to Looe.

On Thursday, December 27th 1860 a special train left Moorswater at 10.30 am and arrived at Looe just after 11 am. This event was described in some detail in the "Western Daily Mercury" of the same date under the heading "Open Day":

"Volunteers of Liskeard in command of Captain Hawker of Menheniot, and Lieutenant Childs, proceeded with their band, headed by Bugle Major Thomas Channon to Moorswater. There were eight open trucks provided by the Company. The morning was wet and cold. Among those present was the Mayor of Liskeard, Edward Geach, Esq., the proprietor and father of all this handiwork, Richard Hingston, Esq., and Thomas Sargent, Esq., Member of the Committee of the Canal and Railway Company. The carriages were decorated with small flags and the engine was also dressed gaily.

"All being ready, the train started and proceeded at a very good pace down the valley. As it progressed, there appeared scores of people on the heights, all of whom set forth an awakening cheer, which was taken up and echoed by those on the train. Here and there a new view opened up on the traveller, and when the trees wear their summer clothing, the valley will present an appearance of beauty not to be surpassed by any of the lovely valleys of Cornwall. We passed the fine town of Duloe, the famous Church and Well of St. Keyne, the virtues of whose waters have been so happily described in lines known by everyone by Southey and thence between the beautiful estates of Trenant and Morval, the respective properties of W. M. Peel, Esq., and J. F. Buller, Esq. A little beyond this the port and harbour of the ancient borough of East and West Looe opened upon us, with the new long bridge that spans the estuary standing in the foreground. The ships were all gaily dressed and everything looked jubilant. At the foot of the bridge of the East Looe side, the entire populations of the boroughs seemed to have congregated and if the number of youthful Looe-ites may be in anyway regarded as a sign of the prosperity of the place, there could be no mistake about it."

To complete the festivities a Public Tea and a Ball were given in the evening. Meanwhile, because of the great upsurge in mineral traffic at that time and the construction of the railway to Looe, the Directors of the Liskeard & Caradon Railway also decided to relay their line and introduce locomotive traction. The terms of the original L. & C. Act of 1843 had forced that company to use horses for hauling the empties and any back traffic up to the Caradon mines but now on May 15th 1860 its intended use of steam locomotives was to be authorised. In the same Act the L. & C. was empowered to regulate its existing capital in the sum of £18,825, comprising £11,625 in whole shares of £25 and the remainder in one third shares of £8 6s 8d while sanction was also given to raise a further £12,000 in new £25 shares and £9,000 by loans. But the most important provisions of the Act empowered the company to make alterations on two portions of its existing railway involving the improvement of the main line between Moorswater and South Caradon together with the realignment of part of the Cheesewring line to improve the inclined plane near Gonamena, involving a line two miles in length from a junction with the main line near Trecarne Farm to Gonamena on the Cheesewring branch. Moreover the company was to build a new branch approximately one mile in length from Crows Nest to Tokenbury Corner, and to purchase, take on lease or arrange for the working of the Kilmar Tramway, belonging to the Cheesewring Granite Company.

All these works gave the Canal Committee the opportunity to dispose of surplus rails and reduce their overspending for on September 5th 1860 it was recorded that they had managed to sell to the L. & C. £842 10s 5d worth of rails at the current market price. By the 1860 Act the Caradon Railway was authorised also to negotiate with the Harbour Commissioners for a further improvement of unloading facilities at Looe including the provision of more sidings if necessary. Five years were allowed for the completion of all the new construction and improvements and as the copper trade was now at its zenith the company was able to declare a dividend of 5% in February 1861. New plans were prepared in 1864 for an extension to West Looe but were not proceeded with.

Although the Canal Committee had been extremely anxious to get the new railway in operation, they were rather dilatory in fixing standard carriage rates even for the main items involved, and it was not until Wednesday, May 1st 1861 that the following were finalised:

From Moorswater to Looe and so in proportion for any less distance	Copper ores	2/6d per ton
	Lead ores	2/6d per ton
	Granite	2/0d per ton
From Looe to Moorswater and so in proportion for any less distance	Mining Coals	2/9d per ton
	House Coals	2/0d per ton

Details of other tolls were decided on June 5th and the main items were as follows:

Limestone	1/od per ton
Culm for burning lime	1/od per ton
Timber	2/od per ton
Iron	2/9d per ton
Brick	2/9d per ton
Manure	2/6d per ton
Sand	1/9d per ton
Building Stone	2/od per ton
Burnt Lime	2/od per ton
Corn	2/3d per score of 20 bushels

Although after the building of the railway to Looe there was ample capacity for the increasing volume of traffic, the additional costs incurred in operating the line meant that the final profit of the Canal Company was little higher than before and this is clearly shown in a comparison of income and expenditure for the years 1858 and 1863. The first shows the tonnage and value of traffic carried by the canal and the second the tonnage and income of the railway:

	1858—Canal		1863—Railway	
	Tons	£	Tons	£
Coal	12,966	934	18,854	2,222
Copper	17,238	862	27,252	3,193
Granite	5,785	217	7,168	717
Limestone	5,214	124	4,159	208
Others	3,301	153	4,779	456
	44,504	2,290	62,212	6,796

Although there was a 30% increase in traffic and a threefold increase in income, with additional operating costs the profit in 1858 of £1,822 was only increased to £2,124 in 1863. The holders of the Old Canal shares continued to receive their 5% dividend but the new shareholders received nothing until the outstanding loans had been paid off.

Although it had been obvious from the outset that it would be extremely advantageous if the two lines from Moorswater were to be operated as one system and provision for working arrangements had been contained in the Liskeard & Looe Railway Act of 1858, little had been done beyond the provision of wagons by the Caradon company and indeed as late as July 3rd 1861 a joint meeting was held to consider the cost of building a satisfactory junction between the lines of the two companies at Moorswater. Nevertheless on December 4th of the same year a preliminary meeting was held to discuss traffic arrangements between the two companies and on March 10th 1862 the Directors of the Caradon Railway and the Canal Committee held a joint meeting at which details of a working agreement were thrashed out. The L. & C. were to charge the Canal £238 for the use of their

Caradon *at Crows Nest with a train of granite in* 1906

wagons for the year ending December 31st 1861, and then one farthing per ton per mile which would also include "oil and grease and repairs". At the same meeting the L. & C. Directors offered to work the Looe line for 1⅛d per ton per mile and this was formally accepted two days later. A variety of tolls for the journey between the Caradon mines and Looe were devised, for example copper ore from Phoenix Road to Looe being carried for 6/3d per ton while in the reverse direction a ton of coal would cost 6/10d from Looe to the Cheesewring.

These arrangements were soon formalised and it was stipulated that the L. & C. would undertake the working of the Looe line for 30 years and would pay to the Canal Company 50% of the gross receipts with a guaranteed minimum of £1,600 per annum. The same year, 1862, saw the arrival of *Caradon*, the first of the three L. & C. six-coupled saddletanks and the ever-increasing traffic led to the purchase of two further locomotives in 1864 and 1869 respectively.

Although abandonment of the canal had not been envisaged in the original scheme, the opening of the railway, parts of which encroached on the formation of the Canal, caused the waterway almost immediately to fall into virtually total disuse, apart from the lower section between Tarras Pill and Sandplace. But although business was confined almost exclusively to the railway, the undertaking remained legally a canal company until 1895, and the Management Committee had to deal with a few tricky problems in the 1860s. The first of these concerned the use of the Crylla Rivulet or Feeder by the Liskeard Waterworks Company to supplement the town water supply. The use of the Crylla Rivulet as a canal feeder had itself caused problems in the early days

22

and the Committee were loth to get involved in fresh controversy. But as the waterway was not drawing much from the Crylla, on December 4th 1861 it was agreed in principle that the waterworks should draw a supply from it although it was not until November 11th 1863 that the Common Seal of the Canal Company was affixed to a Grant of License authorising the Waterworks Company to use the Crylla in perpetuity for a fee of £5 per annum.

But the operation of the lower section of the canal was to cause even greater problems for the Committee; this had been kept open only because of an agreement with a local landowner, Mr Buller of Morval, which allowed toll free access at Tarras Pill, Sandplace and Looe, for his boats or those of his tenants, any other persons being charged 3d a boat. The Committee naturally had tended to neglect the canal which was becoming silted up in parts and in May 1865 Mr Buller made a strong complaint about the condition of the canal quays at Sandplace and Looe particularly as the company was actively involved in improving the facilities at the latter place, the Engineers having been instructed over a year previously to prepare extensions to the railway terminus there. Moreover on November 1st 1865 the Common Seal of the Canal Company was affixed to a conveyance for the transfer from the Duchy of Cornwall for a portion of the Foreshore at Looe Bridge and a licence for dredging out the necessary channels. All this made Mr Buller very angry and in the same month he finally forced the Canal Company to give an undertaking to provide a wharf 350ft in length at Sandplace and to greatly improve the facilities for unloading his boats at Tarras Pill. Gradually, however, the use of this lower section also diminished still further and by 1909 it was estimated that only about 200 tons of sand, seaweed and manure were being carried to this point and this too soon fell into total disuse, so that now only rotting locks and choked sections of stagnant water remain to remind us of this once prosperous waterway.

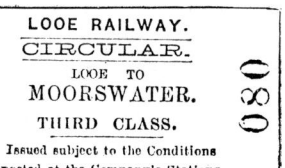

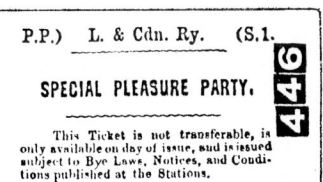

CHAPTER 3

Expansion and Bankruptcy

After the opening of the railway to Looe and the introduction of steam power on the Caradon line, we enter a period of stability and relative prosperity for the railways and above all for the mining industry. The greatest of the mines, South Caradon, had experienced a lean period in the late forties after the opening of the Caradon line, for then there was a temporary drop in the price of copper, and the company had to obtain much needed new equipment, while the purchase of shares in the railway and compensation paid to various landowners for damage caused by mining operations had made further drains on its resources. But regular profits were soon again forthcoming and by the mid-fifties over 600 people found employment there, living in small cottages near the mine and in the area around Tremar, Darite and Pensilva. New and successively larger 40in and 45in pumping engines had been installed to combat the growing influx of water and by 1862 its owners had purchased a 60in engine and two more steam whims for raising ore, while fresh shafts were also being sunk to tap the rich lode at other points, which were connected to the dressing floors by primitive tramways. By 1868 ore worth £1,128,595 had been brought up from the mine, and this had realised a profit of not less than £315,605, while in 1873 alone, 5,230 tons of ore were sold, giving a dividend of £12,288, which calculated on the company's still unchanged nominal capital of £640 had produced an annual return of no less than 1920%. Nevertheless the general depression of the copper mining industry was becoming apparent in the area and in 1874 the West Caradon mine, which had passed its prime in the early sixties and had been partially closed in November 1868, was finally abandoned although a new attempt was made to work it in the early eighties. Craddock Moor, Caradon Consols and the Gonamena mines had also closed, but East Caradon mine on the other hand after a poor beginning struck it rich in 1860, when the longest and richest unbroken course of copper ore ever found in Cornwall was discovered and by 1865 250 people were employed in the 110 fathom deep mine. This was equipped with both 48in and 30in pumping engines and up to 1872 had paid £92,000 in profits. Another late developer was Glasgow Caradon Consols which only became really profitable after 1870 when other mines were all but closed. Although producing ores of relatively poor quality, the Marke Valley mines, a somewhat ramshackle undertaking, continued to be profitable well into the 1870s and even as early as 1855 had a huge 70in pumping engine although it lacked the

Caradon at Cheesewring with a Sunday School outing

usual surface tramways for easy transportation of ore to the dressing floors.

As far as tin mining was concerned, the South Phoenix mine had been the subject of several unsuccessful attempts to promote a profitable undertaking, but the Phoenix United mine, although employing over 450 people in 1864, by which time it had paid over £150,000 in dividends, had almost exhausted its copper deposits and was to turn its main interest to tin mining. By 1870 it had taken over the neighbouring West Phoenix Mine and there were no less than 10 pumping engines in regular use besides several large waterwheels, the largest being 60ft in diameter, while a hydraulic pumping engine was in use underground. As over 550 people were employed there, extensive surface buildings were necessary and tramroads connected the mine with the L. & C. on both sides of the sett.

The heavy rail traffic thus generated was not without its problems for both the Looe and Caradon companies and maintenance of track and rolling stock proved expensive so the L. & C. was forced to ask for a modest increase in its charges and on May 6th 1868 the Canal Committee agreed that this should be fixed at 1¼d per ton per mile. Although profitability was still reasonable, the Canal Company was forced to borrow money from a number of people and the Committee were continually plagued by the various mineowners for reductions in tolls but these were generally turned down although on October 8th 1872, after refusing the applications of the Marke Valley, East Caradon and Glasgow Caradon Consols Mines, the tolls for the South Caradon Mine were reduced by 2d per ton after consultation with the L. & C. Directors.

In the mid seventies after working the Looe line for more than 10 years the Liskeard & Caradon Railway became anxious to lease the newer line and thus tighten its grip on a company which, because of the general uncertainty concerning the future of the copper trade, might prove to be a useful extension of its own activities, particularly in view of the discussion on starting passenger services between Moorswater and Looe. It was felt too that passenger traffic would also help to offset the gradual decline in the gross receipts on the Liskeard & Looe Union Canal Company as this summary of accounts for the years 1869–76 shows:

Year	Gross Receipts £	Expenditure £	Balance to Nett Revenue Account £	% of Gross Receipts
1869	6,245	4,050	2,195	35.0
1870	5,724	3,347	2,377	41.5
1871	5,535	3,346	2,189	39.5
1872	5,347	3,594	1,753	33.0
1873	5,199	2,932	2,267	43.5
1874	4,387	2,566	1,821	41.5
1875	4,374	3,099	1,275	29.0
1876	4,605	3,237	1,368	30.0
TOTAL	41,416	26,171	15,245	Average 36.5

A formal approach by the L. & C. was reviewed by the Canal Committee on August 7th 1877 and after discussion as to the most favourable terms for both companies it was agreed originally that the Canal Company should receive 38 % on the gross receipts, calculated by mileage where merchandise was carried over the lines of both companies, but this payment should not fall below the £1,600 which had been guaranteed under the working agreement and which also represented a 4 % return on the total authorised capital and loans of £40,000. As 38 % of the previous eight years' average revenue was £1,967 and the actual surplus had amounted to £1,905, the fall back figure appeared readily attainable.

The L. & C. entered on the lease of the Looe line from January 29th 1878, and their engineer took possession of the permanent way and works from February 27th of the same year. Under the final terms of the agreement approved in principle at the Special General Meeting of the Canal Proprietors on December 7th 1877, the minimum rental charge had been fixed much lower at £1,350, as this would be sufficient to pay interest on the authorised loan debt of £14,000 while giving shareholders the same dividend as averaged for the past five years. At the end of the first year the L. & C. paid £1,792 9s 10d to the Canal Company, and after all other expenses had been defrayed was able to pay out £1,068 15s 0d in dividends to its own shareholders leaving a surplus of £126 12s 7d to be carried forward for the following year's operations.

But the Directors of the L. & C. were most ambitious and had other schemes for extending their sphere of influence so on November 14th 1877, they had informed the Canal Committee of their plans to extend the Caradon line northwards and also for a connection to the Cornwall Railway at Liskeard which they stressed would be in no way injurious to the Looe line as the benefits to be derived from joining the main railway system of the country were enormous. In the next few years their arguments became even more persuasive, particularly as a passenger service between Moorswater and Looe had begun on September 11th 1879.

In this atmosphere it was obvious that the destinies of the two companies were being drawn closer together and after some informal talks had taken place, a meeting was held on October 7th 1881, between the Canal Committee and the Directors of the L. & C. to discuss the possibilities of amalgamation either by Act of Parliament or by the purchase of one company by the other. The L. & C. Directors also outlined in more detail their scheme for a five mile extension of the Caradon line northwards from a junction on the Kilmar line to a point near Trewint and Five Lanes in the parish of Altarnun at an estimated cost of £3,500 per mile. There was no doubt that the L. & C. intended to be the dominant force in any amalgamation and the Canal Committee felt a certain wariness about this particularly as the prosperity of the Caradon line depended almost exclusively on mineral traffic while the Looe line had yet to realise the full potential of its new and still growing passenger traffic. So they prevaricated by saying they would only entertain the purchase of the Canal if the terms offered by the L. & C. were right and the deal was approved by the Canal proprietors. The Caradon Directors nevertheless pressed on with their scheme for gaining control of their neighbour and persuaded a certain Mr Francis William Fox of Westminster to make an offer for shares in the Liskeard & Looe Union Canal which would be conditional on the latter making the necessary arrangements with the L. & C. Mr Fox made known his intentions to the Canal Committee and on December 6th 1882 offered £42,350 for the Company but, although acceptance of the offer was recommended by the Committee, the financial arrangements which Mr Fox had hoped to make were not forthcoming and the deal fell through.

Meanwhile as the future of the major mines in the Caradon area still seemed reasonably bright despite the generally depressed copper prices, the L. & C. Directors continued with their promotion of new lines to the north of Caradon, and also in finding a way of eliminating the difficult Gonamena incline which was proving a hindrance to the efficient operation of their line despite the improvements carried out some 20 years previously. Thus on July 12th 1882 the Liskeard & Caradon Railway was empowered to construct no less than seven branches totalling some 12 miles in length. These included a line running from Tokenbury Corner around the north side of Caradon Hill to join the original line to the Cheesewring near Minions Mound.

As this would enable the Gonamena Incline to be closed it was soon built and its completion brought the total length of the L. & C. R. to $12\frac{1}{2}$ miles. Sanction was sought for a connection from Moorswater to the Cornwall Railway near Liskeard where a new station was to be built, but this was rejected, although the ambitious extension northward from Sargent's Corner, just south of the Kilmar mine, right across Bodmin Moor to Trewint Marsh, near the main Bodmin–Launceston road, was authorised. The gradients on this latter line were nowhere to exceed 1 in 80 and were generally to be little more than 1 in 100, while on the much flatter upper section the average gradient was to be about 1 in 250 and the last $2\frac{1}{2}$ miles almost level. Work started on the new Trewint line near Kilmar on May 6th 1884, and by June 23rd, $1\frac{1}{4}$ miles had been constructed. Stations were to be built at Lydford Gate, Trewint and Two Bridges and it was estimated that when the line was built the cost of carrying coals would be reduced from 8s by road to only 1/6d. Nevertheless the new line only reached Rushyford Gate and the scheme was never completed nor indeed was the further extension from the proposed terminus of the first line at Trewint Marsh to a junction with the North Cornwall Railway line between Camelford and Launceston for which the L. & C. had obtained authorisation on July 28th 1884, after having informed the Canal

A general view of Moorswater circa 1906

Moorswater station circa 1900

Committee of its intentions in the previous December. On March 11th 1884 the latter had agreed to the insertion of a clause in the L. & C. Bill that the annual payment for the lease of the Looe line would remain at £1,350 but that the Canal Company would receive one half of the passenger revenue from the Moorswater–Looe section while the Caradon Company would enjoy the whole of the receipts generated by the extension from Sargent's Corner to Trewint for the first 10 years after its opening and the same terms would apply to the further extension to the Launceston line.

This latter scheme had been modified from a proposal put forward in November 1882 for a line running from Trewint Marsh near Altarnun to a terminus at Camelford, in a field belonging to the Duke of Cleveland which was bounded by the Camelford–Launceston Road on one side and Trefrew Lane on the other, after following a route through St. Clether, Davidstow and Minster. An extension to Boscastle was also envisaged in the earlier project but was not taken up in the authorised scheme.

But unfortunately the Caradon line's main source of income from the copper mines both in ore and the back traffic of coal was soon to end. Between 1878 and 1886 its gross traffic receipts had fallen from £9,196 13s 3d in 1878 after a peak of £9,876 12s 1d in 1880 to a mere £4,507 15s 11d in 1886, by which time its situation had become so bad that a Receiver, Mr L. C. Foster of Coombe, a former Director of the Company, had been appointed by the Court of Chancery to administer its affairs. The Canal Company, which was one of its principal creditors as the L. & C. was failing to meet its minimum guarantee of £1,350 a year, also found it hard to bear this additional burden and relations between the Directors, shareholders and the Receiver were to become very strained, particularly as after the crash of the Caradon line the Canal Company's overdraft was proving difficult to support. A steady decline in the payment to the L. & L. had been apparent from the outset for, as we have seen, £1,792 was paid on the results of the operation in 1878 but three years later this had fallen to £1,509 and in 1882 only £1,479 was made available by the L. & C. with the downward trend continuing to the inevitable failure to meet its guarantee, and on Friday, October 29th 1886, at a special General Meeting of the Canal Proprietors, it was admitted that the Committee were unable to obtain any money from the Caradon line and they were to take the opinion of Counsel as to the course they should adopt. Yet even at the Annual General Meeting of the L. & C. in February 1882, despite finance for its projected extensions, it was announced that the company would pay 5% dividend on the one third shares and 2½% on both the original and new £25 shares. In the case of the Canal Company, by December of the following year only £700 of the £26,000 authorised share capital remained unissued and all but £650 of the authorised loans had been taken up, so the position was not by any means serious.

To look briefly at the fortunes of the mighty South Caradon mine helps to understand some of the reasons for the rapid decline. As we have seen, in 1870 over 600 people were employed there but although the ore was of very good quality, the gradual decline in the market value of copper had reduced the financial return on each ton of ore produced and as the price the smelters paid fell lower and lower, the mine had to be worked hard not to pay dividends but to merely meet its costs. By 1880 drastic measures were obviously necessary if the mine was to survive, and two years later the adventurers and their families who still retained control of the concern even at this date were told of a proposal to turn it into a limited company to provide new capital for extending the mine and making its operation more profitable. In May 1883, South Caradon Ltd. came into being, bought up the mine and its machinery for £16,000, and invested considerable capital in the following year on improvements, but although almost 8,000 tons of rich ore were brought up in the next two years, with more than 350 people employed, the price obtained for it was so low that it was no longer an economic proposition to continue and the mine was closed in September 1885. The same fate overtook West Caradon, which had been restarted in a small way in 1880, as well as East Caradon and Glasgow Caradon Consols, the inevitable demise of the latter two at the end of 1885 being somewhat hastened by the uncontrollable influx of water when the South Caradon mine stopped pumping.

A sudden but artificial rise in copper prices in 1889 gave brief hopes of a resurgence in the industry but this was followed by an even worse decline and the Caradon area became once more almost deserted save for the residues and abandoned machinery of half a century of mining. Only the Phoenix United Tin Mines, which had seen a brief prosperity

Afternoon mixed train from Moorswater arriving at Looe headed by
Caradon *in* 1900

in the seventies and eighties, and the Granite Quarries provided a precarious livelihood for those remaining and the once bustling mining villages of Pensilva, Darite, St. Cleer and Tremar, which in their heyday had housed several thousands, soon became almost depopulated.

With the voluntary liquidation of the Phoenix United Company in December 1894, tin mining too came virtually to an end in the area, and during the last decade of the nineteenth century the rusting metals of the Liskeard & Caradon Railway saw only an occasional load of granite from the Quarries or a small amount of coal for the Phoenix Mines. Fortunately passenger traffic on the line to Looe continued to flourish and even with the Caradon line merely a liability the two railways managed to eke out an existence until at the turn of the century new impetus was given by the completion of a connection to the main railway system of the country at Liskeard.

CHAPTER 4

The Connection to The Great Western Railway at Liskeard

The possibility of building a connection to the Cornwall Railway's main line at Liskeard had often been discussed and, as we have seen, several schemes had been discussed and indeed in 1882 one had even been laid before Parliament, but none had yet come to fruition. The link line in the 1882 scheme, put forward by Silvanus Jenkin, was to have left the Caradon line to the north of the engine sheds at Moorswater, before passing under the eastern end of the Moorswater Viaduct and rising gradually to cross the Lamellion Road and enter Liskeard station at the west end near the goods shed. Although the scheme in itself was both practical and not very expensive it was rejected by the House of Commons as it was felt that adequate station accommodation could not be provided at Liskeard. Moreover in addition to any difficulties of construction, there was also the break of gauge at Liskeard to be considered, and this may have contributed to a certain lack of interest particularly on the part of the Cornwall Railway and the Great Western Railway with which it was to be amalgamated on June 1st 1889.

However, by the late eighties it had become obvious that the days of the broad gauge were numbered and in 1888 Mr Joseph Thomas. M.I.C.E., a civil engineer living in Looe, put forward the first of several schemes to be devised by him for linking the two local lines to the rest of the British railway system. He was distressed because his home town was apparently dying through the lack of traffic and commerce due to the recent demise of the mines in the Caradon area, and indeed he was also involved in the construction of the Hannafore approach road at West Looe which it was hoped would contribute greatly to the development of Looe as a holiday resort. In view of the number and variety of schemes produced by him to overcome the difficulties of making a link to the main line at Liskeard, it may be thought that Mr Thomas was merely an idealist of limited experience. Nothing could be further from the truth for he had worked extensively on both railway and dock installations in America and Europe and he had been responsible for the construction of the new entrance to the Royal Albert Dock in London. It is indeed a tribute not merely to his engineering skill but also to his perseverance that the connection was eventually completed.

His first scheme envisaged a line running from a point in Moorswater below Landers Mill up the Liskeard Valley to enter the Great Western station at the eastern end, but as this route involved the construction of a large viaduct, it was adjudged much too costly. Not in the least discouraged, two years later Mr Thomas put forward an alternative and rather more practicable scheme. This was to start from Trussell

Bridge and after running through Lodge Hill and Lamellion, would rise by a gradient of 1 in 40 to curve under the embankment at the eastern end of Moorswater Viaduct and run parallel to Liskeard Cemetery, reaching the G.W.R. station by means of a back shunt to join the main line near the goods shed. This scheme, when discussed in greater detail by the Canal Committee in February 1892, was obviously a much more sound proposal but on July 28th it was decided not to recommend its adoption to the Proprietors. Nevertheless on December 8th of the same year after a few very slight modifications had been made, the Committee were much more enthusiastic and it was decided to give it their backing and have the necessary plans made and notices given prior to laying before the House of Commons in the next Parliamentary session. But internal politics prevented any progress being made as the Looe and Caradon Companies, although still locked in a somewhat uneasy working alliance, made more strained by the insolvency of the latter, refused any agreement, still less an amalgamation in order to effect the connection. Efforts were made to interest other parties including the Commissioners of the Port of Looe but no individual or group in the area was either willing or able to raise the necessary capital.

Meanwhile between May 20th and 23rd 1892, the Great Western had finally completed its programme of gauge conversion and the whole of the main line between Plymouth and Penzance was now standard gauge so that one of the major obstacles to a connection at Liskeard had been removed. However, Mr Thomas had become a little disenchanted with this particular junction point and produced a totally new scheme which would in effect involve the construction of a new line from Looe to Menheniot on the G.W. main line. As mentioned before, this small town, some three miles east of Liskeard, had once been a thriving lead mining area with two of its most important mines, Wheal Mary Ann and Wheal Trelawny established by Captain James Clymo, the adventurer of South Caradon. But by the late 1880s all had been closed for large scale production mostly in the previous decade, due to the slump in lead prices, even though in the sixties the discovery of silver in certain of them had led to a minor bonanza in the area.

This new scheme would have started from a junction with the Looe line just above Plashford about half a mile north of Sandplace Halt and then up the Trewidland Valley and under the Liskeard–Morval road at Bye Lane End. From there it would then have run along the west side of Pensipple Farm, crossing the old quarry at Clicker Tor and its adjacent farm, before entering Menheniot station. But to be of any practical use this scheme would have involved the obtaining of running powers over the line between Plashford and Looe and the laying of adequate sidings and connections at the former for the transfer of traffic to and from Liskeard and the Caradon mines. Nevertheless, although this scheme was never laid before Parliament it amply demonstrated that Mr Thomas was not only a competent engineer but a very determined man in his efforts to effect a junction with the main line.

Other schemes mooted about this time involved a hydraulic hoist at Moorswater and yet another solution from Mr Thomas, a centre rack railway on the Riggenbach principle (similar to that running from Vitznau up the Rigi in Switzerland) which would have climbed up from Moorswater at a gradient of 1 in 7. The Board of Trade would not, however, sanction this latter scheme as there would have been no through connection with the main line.

Finally Mr Thomas came up with a scheme which seemed to overcome the manifold difficulties of connecting two stations, about a quarter of a mile apart as the crow flies, but with a difference in altitude of about 150 ft. This involved the construction of a steeply graded line about two miles in length, climbing for much of the distance on a ruling gradient of 1 in 40, which was to describe an almost complete circle in its course as it utilised the contours of the terrain up the slopes of the Bolitho valley. Despite this the junctions at each end of the new line could hardly be called satisfactory for that at Coombe, a short distance south of Moorswater, would face north so that trains to and from Looe were forced to reverse while at Liskeard the new station was to be a terminus at right angles to the main line and access to and from the branch through a siding would not be particularly easy. Plans for this line were laid before Parliament in 1895, after £3,000 to meet the necessary expenses had been collected with some difficulty, but although the Liskeard & Looe Railway Extension Act received the Royal Assent on July 6th 1895, financial problems prevented the speedy construction of the new connection which was described as "A railway, one mile seven furlongs and three chains, or thereabout, in length, commencing by a junction with the railway of the Company (i.e. the Liskeard & Looe Union Canal Company) and terminating at a point 150 yards, or thereabout, measured in a southeastwardly direction from the main entrance to the booking office of the Great Western Railway Company's Liskeard station". Powers were also granted to construct a junction with the G.W. goods siding at Liskeard through which the L. & L. would gain access to the main line. Although the railway from Moorswater to Looe had been opened at the end of 1860, the undertaking had remained legally a canal company until this date when it was empowered to change its name to the Liskeard & Looe Railway Company. It was also authorised to raise additional capital of £30,000 by the issue of New Preference Stock and a further £10,000 by debentures or loans, which coupled with its existing capital of £26,000 and loans of £13,000 increased the total value of the undertaking to almost £80,000. It was estimated at this stage that land purchase, parliamentary expenses, plans and surveys, the construction of the line and the permanent way together with the expenses of the Engineer's supervision, would amount to £19,500 while rolling stock would cost a further £6,500. After the publication of the Looe Company's financial statement for 1896, which showed that 17,044 ordinary and 6,936 excursion passengers had been carried together with no less than 17,265 tons of freight, Mr Thomas set about an analysis of the projected increase of revenue which would accrue from the new connection. Receipts for 1896 had been £687 13s 1d from passenger and parcels traffic and £1,522 18s 8d from freight, a grand total of £2,210 11s 9d. Mr Thomas's estimate of the additional traffic was as follows:

	£ s d
Proportion of traffic now conveyed by boat or road, etc.	2,500 0 0
Excursionists to and from Plymouth (15,000)	500 0 0
Fish from Looe & Polperro (4,000 tons)	400 0 0
Coal (3,000 tons)	375 0 0
Additional local passenger and goods traffic	500 0 0
Traffic from surrounding districts	125 0 0
Development of new Hannafore West Building Estate	300 0 0
	4,700 0 0
Present traffic	2,210 0 0
	6,910 0 0

Estimated cost of 4 trains (3 pass. & 1 goods) Nov.–April	£1,404	
Estimated cost of 5 trains (4 pass. & 1 goods) May–Oct.	£1,755	£3,159
	Balance	3,751 0 0

All these facts were circulated to the shareholders by Mr Thomas on January 26th 1897, with the full backing of the Committee of Management who themselves gave additional information in their own letter on March 12th when they proposed to raise the necessary funds by the issue of 5% Preference Shares with an additional share of the profits to be set aside for further dividends once the necessary $2\frac{1}{2}\%$ had been paid on the original Share Capital of £26,000. Several public meetings were convened by the Committee of Management after the issue of the Prospectus, and at the Special General Meeting of Shareholders on June 15th, 1897, the importance of the scheme was again stressed but a cautionary note was struck when the Committee pointed out that the guaranteed 5% dividend on the £30,000 of Preference Stock authorised by the 1895 Act would be paid only out of profits, and the figure would be reduced to 3% if paid out of capital. Some interest was shown but despite further public meetings both at Looe and Liskeard insufficient of the new shares were taken up to justify beginning work on the new line. A special Report from the Committee of Management to the Shareholders on January 18th 1898, informed them all of the lamentable lack of support and pointed out somewhat forcibly that unless the new connection to Liskeard were built the Company would have to remain dependent on the virtually moribund Caradon line. Undaunted by the general apathy and lack of support

35

for the scheme, Mr Thomas had approached the Great Western Railway to make the connection and if necessary to take over the working of the two lines, but this offer was declined on the grounds that extensive reconstruction of bridges and permanent way on both lines would be necessary if standard G.W. stock were used to operate the system, while the apparently conflicting interests of the local companies would be a further problem. Nevertheless the Great Western maintained good relations with both companies lest the long-abandoned scheme for the extension to the North Cornwall Railway should ever be revived and both lines should fall into the hands of the London & South Western Railway. Having failed with the Great Western Railway, Mr Thomas then asked a well-known firm of contractors, Chambers & Son of Westminster, to inspect the route but they too refused to get involved as they felt the amount of shares taken up was far from sufficient and thus the financial uncertainty was too great for the estimated cost of the project was in the region of £30,000.

After all these fruitless efforts it became apparent to Mr Thomas that whatever reasons may be advanced for not getting involved with the connection to the main line, the underlying cause was undoubtedly money. So, leaving any constructional problems for the present, he had set about finding a financial backer. The Committee's report in January 1898 had contained reference to a firm of London solicitors acting for a gentleman who was willing to purchase both the original and new £25 shares for £6 5s od each, and as an earnest of good faith the Committee were prepared to offer their own shares as they recommended acceptance of the offer. Mr Thomas had spent a lot of time persuading the gentleman, who was identified as Captain John Edmund Philip Spicer, J.P. of Chippenham, that his scheme for a connection to the Great Western main line at Liskeard was both practical and worthwhile, By March 1898 the purchase had been completed and Captain Spicer found himself the owner of the Liskeard & Looe Railway shares to a nominal value in excess of £20,000 out of the original total of £26,000—a somewhat doubtful privilege as it seemed at that time. Once the necessary finance was available, no time was lost in starting work, as only three years had been granted for obtaining the necessary land.

On April 19th 1898, Joseph Thomas was appointed Engineer and S. W. Jenkin & Son were to act as Surveyors, while the contract for the construction of the line was awarded to Mr Charles Lang of Thomas Lang & Son, Contractors, Liskeard, who had been prepared to undertake this task ever since its authorisation. The rails for the construction were on this occasion purchased from the Blaenavon Iron Company.

Only two months later, on Tuesday, June 28th 1898, the first sod was ceremonially cut by Silvanus Jenkin, the Senior Engineer of the Looe Railway, and some fifty men were immediately put to work on its construction. Although the conception of the connecting line and its route was obviously extremely bold, it is only when a more detailed

The branch station at Liskeard, looking towards the buffers, in 1922

study of its construction is made that the careful thought behind it becomes really impressive. It was planned so that cutting and embankments alternated regularly throughout its length, and the material from one cutting could be used for the construction of an embankment in the next section. At its upper end, from where the line passed under the Liskeard Viaduct, its course described an arc of 270 degrees on an 8 chain radius. At its lower end at Coombe where a level crossing gave access to Coombe house, the remains of the old canal were diverted and the original channel filled in for some distance to carry the new line.

Construction began on three cuttings at Heathlands Lane, Lodge Hill and Gut Lane on August 1st 1898, the first being completed on July 4th 1900, while the overbridge there had been built earlier, as had the one carrying the line over Coombe Lane. The Gut Lane cutting was finished on August 9th, but the deep cutting at Lodge Hill had to be cut through solid rock and was not complete until November. It was on this section, one of the deepest cuttings in Cornwall, that the only fatality of the construction occurred, when a young labourer was killed by a fall of rock. Work on the other cuttings at Trevillis and Bolitho, which presented fewer problems, had begun on September 1st and October 1st 1898, respectively and these were finished on June 6th and August 9th of the following year. During the construction of the Bolitho cutting a landslip occurred and 5,000 cu yds of earth had to be tipped onto the embankment under Liskeard Viaduct making it considerably wider than originally envisaged. In actual fact, some

37

160,000 cu yds of spoil were excavated from the cuttings and approximately 192,000 cu yds used in the construction of the embankments so the virtue of the method used is very evident.

Work began on the station and goods yard at Liskeard in May 1899 and, when completed on September 15th of the following year, the latter was the second largest in Cornwall, exceeded only by that at Truro. The L. & L. passenger station at Liskeard consisted of a single wood and stone building 202ft in length which housed all the usual offices as well as having a large canopy providing cover for its full length. At Coombe, too, a new platform and shelter were erected, and sidings laid in to cater for the reversal of all trains between Looe and Liskeard necessitated by the formation of the new junction. A new 100ft carriage shed and a 30ft engine shed were built at Looe where the original station was also extensively rebuilt in preparation for the increased traffic envisaged, and the immediate area made more attractive by a garden and lawn in front of the station.

At this time too, discussions were taking place between the Looe and Caradon companies in preparation for the former to take over once more the working of its own line and a lease of the now almost defunct mineral line to Caradon and the Cheesewring. In preparation for this, the Directors of the Liskeard & Looe Railway appointed as Traffic Manager, and later as Superintendent of the Line, Mr Horace H. Holbrook, who had previously been employed on the Great Eastern Railway. He arrived in Cornwall in 1900 and by the time the new connection was completed he had recruited several of his former colleagues from the Great Eastern to work on his new lines, including

Coombe Junction in 1922, looking towards Moorswater

38

Mr A. Burridge who was to be stationmaster at Liskeard. New rolling stock and a new locomotive had also been purchased for the occasion, through the generosity of Captain Spicer whose offer had been accepted on October 11th 1900; these items will be dealt with more fully in Chapter Six.

After a rigorous inspection of all works by the Board of Trade Inspector, including the "Tyers Patent Automatic Train Ticket Apparatus", installed in the signal boxes at Coombe and Liskeard, the line was taken into use for freight traffic on February 25th 1901, but passenger traffic did not begin until nearly three months later. The official opening took place on May 15th of the same year but on May 9th a special train of the old Caradon coaches hauled by the new locomotive *Looe* left Looe for Liskeard at 8.35 am, arriving there at 9.10 am, despite a seven minute climb from Coombe Junction. Other special trains during the day were well patronised and in the six days before the formal opening, the line carried 991 passengers, 257 tons of coal and granite and over 11 tons of small goods despite a shortage of trucks. Nevertheless the opening ceremony and the events that followed are worth recording in some detail. At 1.00 pm on May 15th 1901, amid the explosions of some sixteen detonators, a special train left Liskeard conveying, among others, the Directors and Officials of the Liskeard & Looe Railway, the Mayor of Liskeard, Mr Thomas, Mr Lang the Contractor, and Mr Holbrook the Traffic Manager, who was in charge of the train which consisted of the new American style coaches hauled by *Looe*. No stops were made at intermediate stations, and the train arrived at Looe to a further barrage of detonators while the crowds on the station included representatives of all the public bodies of the twin townships headed by Mr Reginald A. Peter, J.P., Chairman of the Harbour Commissioners. Everyone then formed a procession and marched through the town to Church End, then back to the Guildhall where numerous speeches were made, after which there was a Public Luncheon in a marquee on the Quay at East Looe, when Mr Thomas was presented with a silver bowl in recognition of his services to the town of Looe, and not least to the Harbour Board. These tributes were very timely for unfortunately Mr Thomas died in the following August. The lengthy speeches were reported in the Cornish Times on the following Saturday and the position of the line before the connection was constructed was aptly summed up as "a railway that ran to nowhere and met nothing".

Not including those who travelled by the inaugural special, over 400 passengers were booked from Liskeard to Looe, no less than 260 travelling by the 2.20 pm from Liskeard. Among the many visitors were a party of some 30 or 40 people from Plymouth who had an anxious end to an otherwise auspicious day. They had left Looe on the 8.35 pm train in plenty of time to catch the 9.23 pm from Liskeard to Plymouth (Millbay) but the engine ran out of steam while climbing the bank from Coombe and came to a dead stop. A messenger was sent back to the junction to get another engine from Moorswater, but although only

20 minutes were lost the passengers did not reach Liskeard until almost quarter to ten only to find that their train had gone. There were consternation and a number of them were trying to hire a coach to get them home when Mr Holbrook arrived on the last train from Looe. He had a quick word with the G.W. stationmaster who said he was willing to arrange for the 10.26 pm arrival from Plymouth to return there as a special, which it did, leaving Liskeard at 10.45. The Liskeard & Looe Railway met the entire cost of the special train but undoubtedly made many friends by this prompt action.

The original station at Moorswater was closed on May 15th 1901, and on the same day Coombe Junction, which up till that time had been merely an "exchange" platform for the three-quarter mile walk to the G.W. station, was upgraded to the status of a full station. From the opening of the line until May 31st, no less than 5,133 passengers were carried over the new connection while at Looe large quantities of cattle, hay and bark were loaded for transport to various destinations on the Great Western Railway system.

Changes had also taken place in the balance of power between the Caradon and Looe Railways for the latter, which had been worked by the L. & C. since 1862 and leased by it since January 29th 1878, had now resumed possession of its own line and on May 8th 1901, obtained the complete rolling stock of the L. & C. by compulsory purchase as well as a lease of the mineral line under the terms of the 1895 Act.

But although in the eight years from 1900 passenger traffic over the line to Looe was to more than treble, the Caradon line was most definitely in decline and in 1902 the Liskeard & Caradon Railway had to make payment of £227 4s 2d to the Looe Company to make up its guarantee due to loss of traffic on the Caradon section. In fact this was causing the L. & L. extreme embarrassment and on January 14th of the same year its shareholders had to be informed of the need to approach the Board of Trade for authority to raise further capital of £24,000, £18,000 by the issue of Preference Shares and £6,000 by debentures or loans. This arrangement was confirmed by the Liskeard & Looe Railway Certificate, 1902.

Even though the Caradon line was now leased and worked by the Looe Railway, it was often felt that its condition was no concern of the latter and because of the negligible traffic now originating on it, little was done to improve it or even keep it in a satisfactory state of repair. As the copper mines had all closed, leaving only a very small quantity of tin and granite as a source of traffic, the financial position of the Caradon company was precarious to say the least, and as the Looe company was one of the principal creditors and had not the slightest chance of obtaining repayment in full of any debts, its own financial situation was far from reassuring. Thus the Directors were forced to seek a drastic solution which virtually involved the offloading of the L. & C. onto someone else even if this move brought with it a certain loss of independence as far as the Liskeard & Looe Railway itself was concerned.

*No. 4559 arriving at Lis-
keard with a passenger
train from Looe
in 1955*

CHAPTER 5

Under Great Western Ownership

The Great Western Railway was the logical choice for the Liskeard & Looe Railway to approach for any kind of solution to its problems and as the major company was obviously encouraged by the great increase in passenger traffic over the Looe line, very friendly discussions took place and by an agreement dated August 8th 1907, it was stipulated that the G.W. should take over the working of the Looe and Caradon lines from January 1st 1909, for between 66 and 72% of the gross receipts, while guaranteeing a minimum annual payment of £1,200 to the Liskeard & Looe Railway. At a Special General Meeting of the L. & L. shareholders on Monday, December 12th 1908, it was formally agreed that while the Caradon line would be vested in the G.W. the Looe line would merely be worked by the major company and remain a separate entity. There arrangements were formally authorised by the Great Western, Liskeard & Looe and Liskeard & Caradon Railways Act of May 25th 1909, which vested the 12 miles 60 chains of the Liskeard & Caradon Railway in the G.W.R. as from July 1st 1909, and confirmed the working agreement between the G.W. and the L. & L. companies from January 1st 1909. As mentioned in a previous chapter the brief prosperity of the Caradon copper mines had come to an end in the late 1880s due to the fall in the world price of copper when vast new deposits had been discovered overseas. By 1890 all the major copper mines were closed and only the tin mines and granite quarries eked out a precarious existence. In fact tin mining was also virtually extinct in the area by the same date and only a brief resurgence in the first decade of the present century gave new hope for the Caradon line. The South Phoenix mine had been reopened and a vain attempt was made to work the southerly lodes between 1906 and 1910 but the project ended in failure. Nevertheless in 1907 mine and quarry owners in the Cheesewring area had approached the Plymouth, Devonport & South Western Junction Railway, whose Bere Alston–Callington line was nearing completion, requesting an extension to serve their mines. The P.D.S.W.J. directors very wisely said they could not undertake the construction of such a line but added that they might be interested in working one if such a line were built privately.

On the face of it the reopening of the great Phoenix United mine at approximately the same date after having been virtually disused for some twenty years was a more viable proposition. In the seventies and eighties of the previous century this had been one of the major tin producers of Cornwall and at the start of the new venture in 1908 capital of £100,000 had been made available and a mighty 80in pumping engine was installed which it was estimated would easily keep the mine free from the ever-present danger of flooding. A new shaft was sunk at this time and its depth was increased from 755ft in 1910 to 1,200ft by the summer of 1913, but by this time it was obvious that even the power of the huge pumping engine was insufficient to keep the water level down and underground auxiliary pumps had to be installed.

It is important to realise that throughout this long period of tremendous expense no ore of real commercial value had been brought to the surface despite the existence of a 20ft lode and the company was thus obviously in a precarious financial position. The original £100,000 and a further sum of £40,000 had been spent solely to sink the shaft and provide equipment for the venture. Nevertheless, it was then estimated that a further £60,000 would be necessary for exploration and the provision of adequate water clearance despite all the pumps so far installed. But the First World War was to intervene before new capital could be obtained. Work ceased in August 1914 and as by October all equipment had been brought to the surface it was obvious that no further work was envisaged and thus the last major mine in the Caradon area had finally closed although hopes were raised in 1922 that it might reopen with the aid of a Government grant. Nevertheless the fact that a company with seemingly adequate capital and the most modern equipment available at the time could not make a viable proposition of mining in the Caradon area had been truly discouraging and no further attempts of note were made there.

This closure sounded the death knell of the Caradon line for although traffic from Phoenix United had been somewhat sporadic, there now remained only a diminishing amount of granite from the Cheesewring Quarries and after the daily freights had dwindled to one on only three days a week the Great Western decided that it was no longer worthwhile to continue operations particularly in view of the wartime economies it was being forced to make. Thus from January 1st 1917 the Caradon line was closed completely north of Moorswater sheds, a total of 12 miles, 45 chains, only the 15 chains between the L. & C. sheds and the site of Moorswater station remaining open. Because of the need for steel in essential war industries the line had been completely lifted by April of the same year as the original *raison d'être* of the railway from Caradon to Looe had vanished for ever, although complete abandonment of the line was not formally authorised until the Great Western Railway Act of 1931. The Liskeard & Looe Railway however remained nominally independent for almost 15 years after it had rid itself of the Caradon line but under the provisions of the Railways Act of 1921 it too finally ended up in the hands of the Great Western Railway. At a Special General Meeting of its shareholders on December 12th 1922 formal approval was given to its absorption by the G.W.R. on the following basis. Each £100 3½% debenture was to be exchanged for £87 10s 0d of 4% G.W.R. debenture

43

stock, while each of the £100 5% new preference shares was to be exchanged for £34 4s 1d in cash. The ordinary shares of the company were to be cancelled and the formal vesting of the Liskeard & Looe Railway in the Great Western Railway became effective from January 1st 1923.

Traffic on the line between Liskeard and Looe had continued to increase both in the last decade of independence and under Great Western ownership but the awkward junctions at the former place and at Coombe had precluded the successful running of through trains to Looe and had also impeded the speedy transfer of freight so an alternative route was felt to be necessary. As we have seen, the physical obstacles at Liskeard made it virtually impossible to find a viable solution there at reasonable cost so in the 1930s thought was given to providing a completely new line to Looe.

It was announced by the Government in November 1935 that some £30 million was to be made available to the various railway companies for electrification projects, new lines and improvements to existing routes, as part of a scheme to assist British industries to recover from the world-wide trade depression. The G.W.R. included among its schemes which were authorised under the Great Western Railway (Additional Powers) Act of 1936, a completely new 7 mile line to Looe which was to leave the main Plymouth–Truro line about $1\frac{3}{4}$ miles west of St. Germans station, at a point known as Trerule Foot. This was not the first scheme for a line to Looe from a point other than Liskeard as one of Mr Thomas's many schemes in the 1890s had been intended to join the main line near Menheniot. The new line would head from St. Germans directly towards the sea along the Hessenford Valley before continuing for some three miles along the coast to a terminus on the high ground at East Looe, south of the existing terminus of the branch from Liskeard. Intermediate stations were to be provided at Hessenford, Seaton Beach (near Downderry) and Millendreath while a new hotel and golf course were also included in the scheme.

The projected branch involved some extremely heavy engineering work between Looe and Keveral, including two masonry viaducts, the first at Millendreath 123ft above river level with nine 70ft and three 35ft spans, and the second near Keveral 144ft above river level with eleven 70ft and two 35ft spans. Two tunnels were also necessary in the four miles near Looe, one of 700yds at Looe and the other west of Downderry, 2,288yds in length, for which it was intended to bore three shafts to enable eight faces to be worked simultaneously. Smaller engineering work included three bridges and five culverts while yet another long tunnel would be required near St. Germans. It was planned to operate direct services between Looe and Plymouth using the new streamlined diesel railcars which would cover the distance in 35 minutes, thus reducing the journey time by half an hour compared with the existing route via Liskeard.

The first construction contract was to be for the four mile section

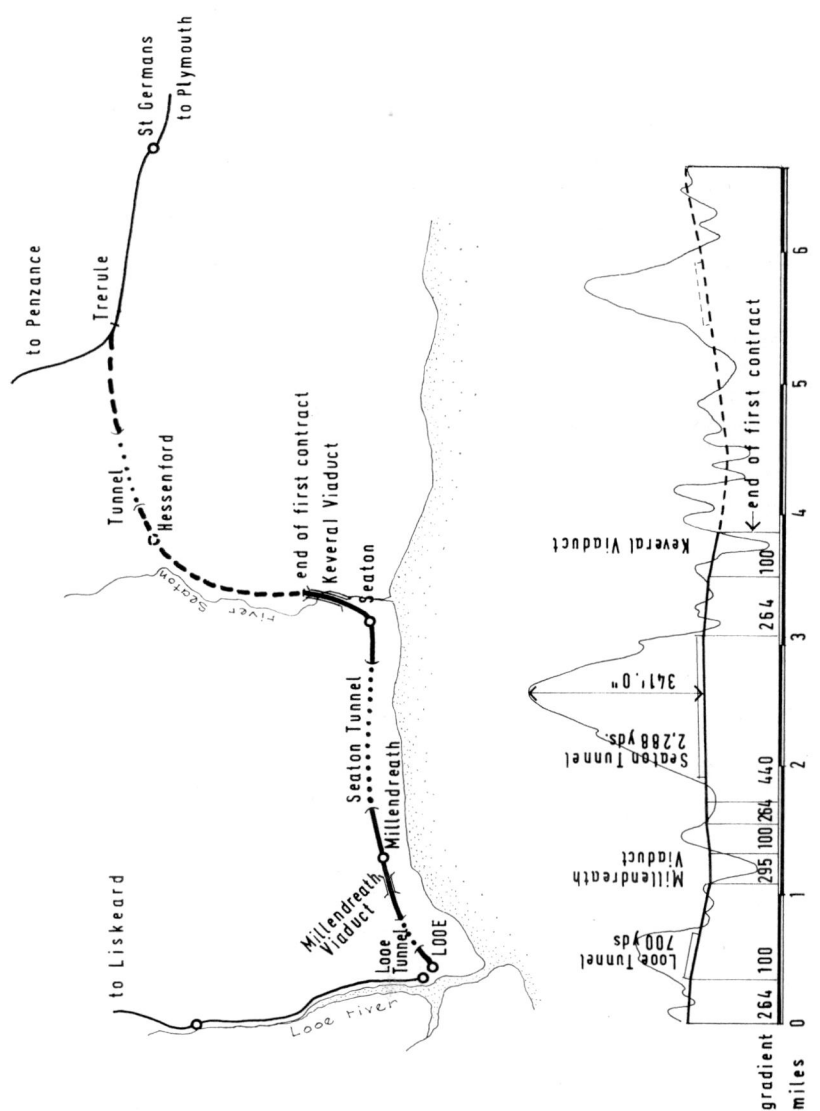

The proposed new line of 1935

from Looe to the north end of the Keveral Viaduct which included both viaducts and two long tunnels as well as a new road leading from Polliscourt to the site of the new Great Western Railway hotel. Preliminary work for the new line, involving the setting out of the centre line, began in the autumn of 1937, but had to be carried out under extreme difficulties due to the thick undergrowth and the hilly nature of the terrain involved. Four test shafts were bored by Messrs C. Isler & Co. Ltd. of Southwark and it was estimated that some 700,000 cu yds of excavation would be necessary during the construction of tunnels and cuttings on this section alone. Progress was very slow and at the outbreak of war in 1939 only the golf course, which ran from the site of the new hotel on the cliffs at Millendreath to a point near the present Monkey Sanctuary at Murrayton, had been completed.

Although an extension of time until January 1st 1958 was granted for the scheme's completion, post-war conditions did not permit of its resumption and the British Transport Commission abandoned the project soon after Nationalisation and sold most of the land involved, but even today it is still possible to follow some of the preliminary earthworks at Looe. So the last of the many schemes for an effective alternative to an otherwise insoluble problem was never completed and even now it is still necessary to change stations at Liskeard and reverse at Coombe to reach Looe.

CHAPTER 6

Locomotives and Rolling Stock

As the 1843 Act incorporating the Liskeard & Caradon Railway had specifically forbidden the use of locomotive engines, its early rolling stock consisted only of wagons for carrying ore and granite from the mines and quarries to the canal, and coal, fertiliser and some general merchandise as a back cargo. These were generally of 6 ton capacity and fitted with screw brakes for gravity working on the down journey, although at the opening of the line it was stated that there was one wagon "on eight wheels, of very superior construction" for carrying heavy loads of granite. Horses which were housed mainly at Moorswater were used to haul the trucks back up to Caradon. But as traffic increased, this mode of operation became less and less satisfactory and in the late 1850s when the Canal Company was contemplating the construction of its railway to Looe, the Directors of the L. & C. began to think in terms of modernisation of their route and repeal of the clause in the original Act which prevented them from using locomotive power. In 1859 they asked the intentions of the Canal Committee on this score and on September 7th the latter stated at one of their meetings "it is the intention of the Canal Company to work the line by steam power at the earliest possible convenient time".

Because of the rather difficult financial position of the Canal Company at this time nothing was done to provide rolling stock for the new line for some months and early in May 1860 the Engineers had to urge the Committee to obtain an engine and carriages as soon as possible. Negotiations had in fact been taking place with the Liskeard & Caradon Railway on this very subject and at the Committee Meeting on May 7th it was made known that the Canal Company would supply the locomotive and the Caradon Company the wagons, augmenting the existing fleet where necessary as eight days later authority was granted to the latter to use steam locomotives on its own line.

Messrs Jenkins & Trathan were then instructed to obtain quotations for a locomotive to work the Looe line and on October 23rd 1860, a letter dated three days previously, from a contractor, James Murphy of the Railway Works, Newport, Mon., was read to the Canal Committee. In it Mr Murphy offered to hire an engine at a fixed minimum daily rate of 30 miles at 2s od per mile, or £3 a day, all mileage above the minimum to be paid for at the same rate. The cost of transporting the locomotive from Newport to Moorswater was to be borne by the Canal Committee who were also to supply the engine with water and coal and provide an engine shed and coal enclosure for its use. Mr Murphy also offered the Canal Company the option of purchasing

47

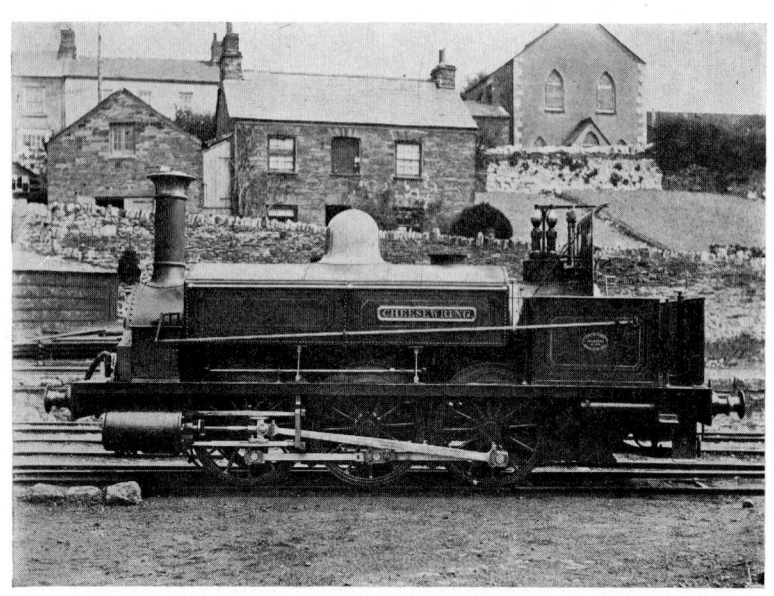

Liskeard and Caradon Railway locomotives at Moorswater

Above: Cheesewring   *Below:* Kilmar

the engine within 12 months for a sum not exceeding £700. The agreement to hire the locomotive, which was described as a tank engine, was completed on December 5th and it arrived at Moorswater on December 26th 1860, after having been brought down from Liskeard station by a team of 28 horses. Little definite is known of this locomotive which was named *Liskeard* although it is possible that it was an 0-6-0 tank weighing 15 tons in working order. During the next few months it was decided to purchase *Liskeard* outright and a meeting with Mr Murphy produced a Memorandum of Proposed Agreement for Purchase of the Engine *Liskeard*, dated September 13th 1861, in which it was stated that the Canal Company would pay Mr Murphy the sum of £600 for the engine and take possession of it from the end of the week, while the stocks of coal, spare parts and other stores were to be valued. As we have seen in Chapter Two, in March of the following year the Liskeard & Caradon took over the working of the Looe line and the Committee offered *Liskeard* to the former for £600. This was taken over to work the line but when some five months later the first of their own engines arrived, the L. & C. Directors were anxious to dispose of it as it was in need of repair. It was nevertheless used sporadically for the next three or four years, despite the arrival of a second new engine in 1864, and it was finally sold back to Mr Murphy in August 1866.

During the forty years that the L. & C. was responsible for working both Looe and Caradon lines, it owned only three other locomotives, all built by the same company to a basically similar design. The first of these, *Caradon* was obtained from Gilkes, Wilson & Co. of Middlesbrough (Works No. 138) in 1862 and was an 0-6-0 saddle tank with 13in × 24in outside cylinders, 4ft 0in coupled wheels of which the driving pair were flangeless, and working pressure of 140 lb/in^2. Illustrations show this as having a round section saddle tank and as there was no bunker coal was carried on the left side of the footplate. It is believed to have received a new firebox, and possibly a boiler, from the Avonside Engine Co. of Bristol in 1878, and was again rebuilt in 1899, being withdrawn in 1907. The firebox wrapper sheet with the inner firebox removed was kept at Moorswater where in 1936 it was mounted over a swiftly flowing stream and provided with a rough seat to form very primitive toilet facilities for the shed staff. Although left in position after the closure and demolition of the old L. & C. shed, it has recently been removed for preservation at the Great Western Society depot in Bodmin.

The second engine *Cheesewring*, also came from Gilkes, Wilson & Co. (Works No. 195) in 1864 but, although the main dimensions were similar to those of *Caradon* with a wheelbase of 4ft 4in + 4ft 4in, this was a long-boiler 0-6-0ST with a squarish section tank, and the trailing set of coupled wheels as drivers although the middle set were flangeless. It was rebuilt in 1890 with a boiler which had a dome on the middle ring and a 700 gallon tank fitted over the barrel only. A general overhaul at Swindon in December 1907 made no real difference to its appearance and its pressure remained at 140 lb/in^2 with a weight in working order of 28 tons 5 cwt. On its acquisition by the Great Western in 1909 it became No. 1311 and finished its active life in the London area. Not surprisingly the Old Oak Common crews were far from enamoured by the very slightly curved weatherboard which formed its only protection against the elements. It remained there throughout the first World War working mainly in a munitions factory at Greenford and was withdrawn in August 1919.

Kilmar was the last of the L. & C. engines and was built by Hopkins, Gilkes & Co. (successors to Gilkes, Wilson & Co.) in 1869 (Works No. 264) to the same basic dimensions as *Cheesewring*. It is probable that it received a new boiler from the Vulcan Foundry in 1887 and was extensively overhauled in Bristol by the Avonside Engine Co. between September 1902 and March 1903, when the large totally enclosed cab which it carried in its latter days was most probably fitted. Its dome was on the back ring of the boiler although the short saddletank fitted between this and the smokebox gave it the appearance of having the dome fitted on the firebox. After a general overhaul at Swindon in December 1908 its boiler pressure remained at 140 lb/in^2 and its weight in working order at that time was given as 22 tons 11 cwt empty and 28 tons 7 cwt full. It became No. 1312 in Great Western stock in the following year and was withdrawn in May 1914.

In the late 1860s the mineral traffic from the Caradon area was at its height and from time to time difficulties were obviously experienced in carrying all the traffic with the two locomotives then owned by the L. & C. and from 1868 to 1871 the stock returns show an extra engine on the books which was obviously needed before *Kilmar* was fully operational. This left the line some time in 1872 and no definite evidence exists of its identity although it was probably hired from the Avonside Engine Co. which did most of the work for the L. & C. at this time. Other locomotive data in the last years of the 19th century is scarce but in 1885 with *Caradon* awaiting repair, and *Kilmar* broken down, an engine was hired from Peckett & Sons, an 0-6-0ST saddletank (Works No. 444) with 14in × 20in outside cylinders. The closure of the Caradon Mines shortly afterwards removed the need for any additional motive power and it was returned to its owners in September 1886. When no engine was available, horses were occasionally used on the passenger service between Moorswater and Looe.

The L. & C. accounts for 1873-7 show an unvarying number of 44 goods wagons and 4 timber trucks in service but during 1878 the number of the former had dropped to 32 but the number of timber trucks had increased from 4 to 8. To operate the passenger service between Moorswater and Looe which began on September 11th 1879, the Caradon company had purchased four completely new vehicles, and these were painted in a dark reddish brown livery with both the inscription "L. & C. R." and the number below in gold letters. There were two brake vans (Nos. 1 and 4) and two four wheel coaches; a three compartment 1st, 2nd and 3rd composite (No. 3) and a four

Looe: (*above*) *off the road at Coombe and* (*below*) *as Port of London Authority No.* 11

compartment 3rd (No. 2) built by the Metropolitan Railway Carriage & Wagon Company at Saltley in 1878 and 1880 respectively. The first class section of the composite had dark blue cloth upholstery but for the second class American cloth was used, while the third class, which was also a smoking compartment had no upholstery at all. By 1899 the third class coach had been modified to an open third but once again only wooden seats were provided for its passengers. From the company accounts for 1885-6 it would appear that another composite coach had been purchased by this time and all these survived until the turn of the century. At the same date in addition to the three locomotives, the company possessed 35 goods wagons, one covered wagon and 8 timber trucks. The goods wagons, which were still generally of 6-ton capacity with footboards and screwdown brakes for gravity working, were also used to carry the intrepid passengers on the Caradon line well and truly at their own risk. For the opening of the new connection to Liskeard at the turn of the century when a more intensive passenger service was to be run, the Liskeard & Looe Railway Directors, about to take over once more the working of the line to Looe, decided to obtain a new locomotive and new rolling stock for which, as we have seen, Captain Spicer put up the purchase money. The locomotive, appropriately named *Looe* was purchased in April 1901 from Robert Stephenson & Co. of Newcastle (Works No. 3050). It was one of that company's standard inside frame 0-6-0 saddletanks with 3ft 6in wheels, 16in × 20in outside cylinders, a working pressure of 130 lb/in^2 and a tank capable of holding 700 gallons. Although able to haul the heaviest trains up the 1 in 40 incline from Coombe to Liskeard, it became derailed on its first visit to Looe. But this was not the end of its misdeeds for on May 22nd 1901, it had just arrived at Coombe Junction with the 8.35 pm from Looe, and was running round its train, when it ran over some points, passed a ground disc signal and was derailed, although this was really the fault of the driver who did not pay attention to the signals. An engine was quickly sent from Moorswater but because the fire was too low it could only take half the train on to Liskeard and had to return to pick up the rest of the passengers.* It arrived in Liskeard at 9.50 pm and made the 9.30 pm train to Looe half an hour late in departure. In fact much of the track between Coombe and Looe was very light and poorly laid so it was soon decided that this locomotive, with its 8ft wheelbase, would be generally too heavy for satisfactory operation on the system and it was sold in April 1902 to the London & India Docks Railway (now the Port of London Authority) where it became No. 11 and survived until December 1950.

To replace this the company purchased another engine, an Andrew Barclay inside cylinder 2-4-0 side tank (Works No. 956) which arrived in 1902 and proved much more successful. Named *Lady Margaret* in honour of the wife of Captain Spicer (later Sir Edmund Spicer) who had financed the new connection to Liskeard, it had 4ft 0in driving

* For a contemporary account of this episode see page 80.

Lady Margaret *at Looe in* 1905

wheels, 2ft 7½in leading wheels, 14½in × 22in cylinders and a working pressure of 160 lb/in². It was provided with an overall cab and had a tank capacity of 560 gallons, weighing 28 tons in working order. It was numbered 1308 by the Great Western and that company's documents show minor variations of its dimensions at different times. On Boiler Diagram J it is shown as having 140 lb/in² pressure, a tank capacity of 500 gallons and leading wheels of 2ft 8in while its weight in working order is given as 25 tons 19 cwt (empty) and 29 tons 16 cwt (full). This would appear to indicate reboilering although it was not until May 1929 in the course of a general overhaul at Swindon that it was given a top feed boiler of similar dimensions, which gave it a typically Great Western appearance. On Boiler Diagram U its weight in working order is given as 28 tons 3 cwt (empty) and 32 tons 0 cwt (full).

Although *Lady Margaret* was quite successful on the Looe line it remained there only until just before the Grouping when it was transferred to the Cambrian section, being shedded at Oswestry until its withdrawal in May 1948 apart from a short time on the Culm Valley line between Tiverton Junction and Hemyock, immediately after its visit to Swindon in 1929, where it established a reputation as a capable and free-steaming engine.

The general locomotive livery at the turn of the century was described as light green, with brown frames lined out in black and yellow. *Lady Margaret*, however, had black frames and was lined out in black and red on the tanks and yellow on the frames, while *Looe* had brown frames with red lining. At this time, these two and *Kilmar* had painted domes, the latter also having a copper-rimmed chimney while *Caradon* and *Cheesewring* had polished brass domes.

The three vacuum brake fitted carriages obtained from Hurst

Nelson & Co. Ltd. of Motherwell for the opening of the new connection to Liskeard in 1901 are of particular interest although their working life was extremely short due to an accident in 1906 which will be described later. One was a 1st and 2nd composite with a guard's compartment and the other two 3rd Class coaches, one of which also contained a guard's compartment.

All three were open saloon bogie coaches, constructed to an American design similar to vehicles then in service in New York. As there were no interior compartments side doors were felt to be unnecessary and entrance was effected from a verandah-like platform at each end of the coach. The seats were placed close to the windows, each seating four people back to back and there were ten windows on each side of the carriage, seven fixed and three sliding. The overall length of each vehicle, which was built on pitch pine underframes, was 40ft and the oak body was 30ft long with an interior height of 6ft 7in. The floors and roof were also of pitch pine while the carriages were panelled inside with alternate strips of pitch pine and sequoia to give decorative bands of dark and light wood. Ceilings were painted white and brass lamps provided in each carriage. First class seats were provided with reversible cushions in blue cloth, picked out with lace while the floors were covered with wax cloth and each window had tapestry curtains sliding on brass rods. In the second class the reversible horse hair cushions were covered with what was officially termed "French carpet" and luggage nets were provided in both sections. Even in the third

Lady Margaret *as G.W.R. No. 1308 before reboilering, but with built-up bunker and new safety valve cover*

54

class section the fittings were somewhat less austere than usual with the seats having alternate laths of dark and light wood and fancy trimmed legs, and even curtains made from the strong untwilled linen or cotton known as "duck" sliding on mahogany rods mounted above the windows. With such finely constructed vehicles the L. & L. should have had no problems for many years as they also had the original L. & C. coaches held in reserve to cover emergencies and peak traffic requirements. However, on Friday, June 15th 1906, there occurred the most spectacular accident ever seen on the Looe line which at one fell swoop put paid to most of the rolling stock. On the previous day the Company had provided a special eleven coach train to convey children, teachers and friends of the Looe Wesleyan Sunday School to Liskeard and thence through to Doublebois. This trip and the return to Looe was accomplished without mishap but on Friday afternoon six coaches were returned to Liskeard at the rear of a Looe–Moorswater freight. The carriages were detached at the junction and taken on up the bank by the engine *Kilmar* while the freight continued on its way to Moorswater. The train, driven by a Mr Miller and with Mr J. Horrell as guard, arrived at Liskeard just after 6 pm and *Kilmar* was being uncoupled from the coaches prior to running round and shunting them into a siding, but as the coupling was tight the engine had to ease up before the stock could be disconnected. While doing this it inadvertently gave them a hard push, and the coaches, which were fortunately empty, started run down the steep, sharply curving line towards Coombe Junction. After a vain attempt to stop them by putting stones under the wheels, it was realised with some horror that the 6.00 pm passenger train from Looe was shortly due at Coombe Junction. The porter-signalman at Liskeard, Mr Husband, just managed to get through to the box at the junction and have the signals and points set against the passenger train so that the runaway could run through to Moorswater, as this was the safest thing to do in the short time available.

Almost immediately the coaches came hurtling down the bank at an estimated 60–70 mph, staying on the rails quite miraculously as they took the points at Coombe, before careering off in the direction of Moorswater with nothing more anyone could do except hope, as their was no means of knowing how the various sets of points were set in the yard or at the locomotive and carriage shed. Luckily work on that day had finished promptly at 5 pm and there was nobody about as the runaways crashed headlong into the carriage shed. Two Hurst Nelson coaches in the sheds and other vehicles standing outside after repair were reduced virtually to matchwood and several others badly damaged, but although strange to relate some of the runaways were not too badly damaged, the buffer springs and draw bars were broken and all were later scrapped.

In such a moment of tragedy, albeit without loss of life, the L. & L. were also somewhat financially embarrassed and, as it needed new coaches quickly at a bargain price, some secondhand vehicles were

Liskeard & Caradon rolling stock at Looe
Left to right, passenger brake van No. 8, four compartment third, three compartment composite (1st 2nd) and passenger van.

Lady Margaret *about to pass under Liskeard Viaduct with a train of the Hurst Nelson coaches*

purchased from the Mersey Railway, which had recently been electrified. These were four wheel vehicles built between 1885 and 1891 by the Ashbury Carriage Co. and obtained at prices between £85 and £95 each. These continued in service until after the working of the line was taken over by the G.W.R. in 1909, and the survivors of the original L. & C. coaches were sold to a contractor for use on miners' trains at a colliery in the North of England. All these were replaced by often equally ancient G.W. stock, a variety of which was employed until 1935 when two new two-coach sets of compartment stock ("B" sets) were provided for use on the branch. Even with four locomotives, the L. & L. was often short of motive power and was forced to hire a locomotive from the G.W. and between 1901 and 1908 this was usually a 4-4-0 saddletank, No. 13, which had been originally built as a 2-4-2 tank in 1886 but converted to the new wheel arrangement in 1897. This had 4ft 1½in coupled wheels, 2ft 8in bogies, 16in × 21in inside cylinders and a boiler pressure of 140 lb/in². Although for some time after its rebuilding it had worked on the Highworth branch, it remained on the Looe line almost continuously from 1901 until the Grouping, after which it served as Works shunter at Swindon until its withdrawal in 1926.

When the Great Western took over the running of the line in 1909, a full inventory of locomotives, rolling stock and the minutest items of workshop equipment was made and evaluated. A copy of this still survives in the B.T.C. Archives in London and makes fascinating reading, particularly when the differing evaluations of Mr Chambers, acting for the L. & L., Mr G. J. Churchward of the G.W.R. and an independent arbitrator are considered.

These are summarised below:

	Mr Chambers			Mr Churchward			Arbitrator		
	£	s	d	£	s	d	£	s	d
Locomotives	3,000	0	0	1,800	0	0	2,000	0	0
Carriages	1,470	0	0	320	0	0	480	0	0
Wagons	292	10	0	200	0	0	220	0	0
	4,762	10	0	2,320	0	0	2,700	0	0

Of the three locomotives owned at that time, *Cheesewring* and *Kilmar* were valued at £500 each and *Lady Margaret* at £800 by Mr Churchward, with the other evaluations correspondingly higher but it will be noticed that it is with regard to the carriages that the greatest gulf occurs between the L. & L. evaluation and the others. The 16 passenger vehicles which the G.W. inspector, Mr J. M. Llewellyn, describes variously as "useless" or "in very bad condition" are all written down in rather cavalier fashion by Mr Churchward at £20 each. In more detail these are three L. & C. coaches, two 1st and 2nd composite and a 3rd, and 13 described as Mersey Tunnel coaches, comprising one 1st, two 1st and 2nd composite, four brake 3rds, five 3rds and one passenger brake van. To judge from Mr Chambers' evaluation he actually wanted to make a profit on the original purchase price of these vehicles from the newly electrified line while the thirty year old L. & C. coaches would obviously not be of great value. At this time too, there were 50 goods vehicles, again all written off by Mr Churchward at the same value of £4 each but comprising 6 timber trucks, 2 brake vans or covered goods wagons and 42 open goods wagons of which one was still in the course of construction. Detailed specifications were given and indicate that the goods vehicles had oak frames, the tare weight of the timber trucks being 4 tons and of the open wagons between 3 tons 6 cwt and 4 tons 5 cwt, their capacity carrying from 6 to 8 tons and their building dates from 1880 onwards.

As might be expected the Great Western very quickly disposed of the majority of the local company's stock, and although the first of the two L. & C. engines taken over was not withdrawn until 1914, services were worked either by No. 13 or *Lady Margaret* with a steady increase in visits from the standard Dean 0-6-0 pannier tanks and saddletanks of the 1901 and 2021 Classes. A Churchward 0-6-0 saddletank of the 1361 Class from Millbay Docks was tested for service on the line but although it proved powerful enough, its short wheelbase and small driving wheels were not suited to passenger working.

But for at least 30 years before dieselisation the line was worked almost exclusively by Great Western 2-6-2 tanks, at first the Churchward 44xx Class engines with 4ft 1½in driving wheels but these were

G.W.R. No. 13 in the yard at Looe circa 1909

58

5553 outside Moorswater shed in September 1961 (inside is No. 5531) shortly before its closure

gradually replaced by his much more numerous 4ft 7½in 45xx Class locomotives, a design perpetuated by his successor, C. B. Collett. Locomotives to be sub-shedded at Moorswater were originally supplied by St. Blazey shed, but in the mid thirties this duty was taken over by Laira, once again reverting to St. Blazey in the years after Nationalisation. All classes in the "uncoloured" group and the 32xx (later 90xx) Class *Dukedog* 4-4-0s were also permitted on the line but it is unlikely that a *Dukedog* was in fact ever seen at Looe. In 1936 the connecting lines at Liskeard were realigned to allow 57xx Class 0-6-0 pannier tanks to shunt the L. & L. goods yard, but heavier locomotives such as the 94xx Class were officially barred from this duty. Restrictions on working the branch still remained, and the G.W.R. operating instructions for 1939 stated that 8-wheel stock exceeding 63ft 6in × 9ft 5¾in was not allowed between Liskeard and Looe while the banking of passenger trains between Coombe Junction and Liskeard was only permitted during the hours of daylight.

Speed restrictions on the line are 20 mph between Liskeard and Coombe, 25 mph between Coombe and Looe and 15 mph at Coombe where in steam days the single platform caused some complications at busy periods as trains had not only to cross but locomotives had to run round in each direction. The first train ran into the platform and after the engine had run round the train was shunted into the loop to enable the second train to enter the platform. Although these problems could have been reduced if push-and-pull working had been introduced on passenger services, the usual 0-4-2 tanks or 0-6-0 pannier tanks would undoubtedly have had difficulty with the stiff gradients from Coombe to Liskeard for the 2-6-2 tanks which were normally allowed passenger loads of up to 240 tons were themselves limited to 179 tons on this section and to 45 freight wagons on the branch. However, despite the fact that some 45xx Class engines were later fitted for auto-train working in South Wales, this type of operation was never adopted on the Looe line although the 2-6-2 tanks remained at work there until the early sixties.

Clearance tests were carried out with a British Railways Type 2 diesel hydraulic B-B locomotive of the D63xx series (Class 22) on March 4th 1959 and further tests using a diesel multiple unit were conducted on October 6th of the same year, but steam operation was to continue for two years longer. When the branch passenger services were finally taken over by diesel multiple units on September 11th 1961, timings were revised so that the service could be maintained by one unit and thus remove the need for crossing at Coombe. Soon after this freight traffic was taken over by the D63xx series diesels which had a wide route availability and which since the withdrawal of freight services from Looe continued to work china clay traffic to Moorswater. All the remaining locomotives of this class were withdrawn during 1971 and their place has been taken by the Sulzer Type 2 diesels of Class 25.

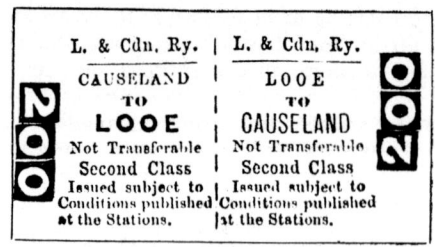

CHAPTER 7

The Lines Described

A traveller to the West Country on the Cornwall main line might well be forgiven if he missed the junction with the Looe line at Liskeard, although he passes high over lines at right angles to the main line both before and after the station. The single terminal platform Liskeard & Looe Railway station is set at right angles to the main line and connection is made through the goods yard via a somewhat tortuous connection which was improved in 1936 to enable through coaches to be worked more easily onto the branch. The site of the once large goods yard is now almost obliterated by some new buildings although long after the demise of steam working a nostalgic note was struck by a notice listing the steam locomotives permitted in the yard and on the branch proper. Leaving the station, the connecting line heads northwards at a relatively gentle 1 in 200 to start on the horseshoe loop which will bring it to Coombe Junction, but soon dips steeply first at 1 in 60 and then at 1 in 40. As the L. & L. station at Liskeard is 335ft above sea level and Coombe Junction a mere 130ft, a descent of 205ft had to be achieved in just over 2 miles. The method of construction using alternate cuttings and embankments, mentioned in a previous chapter, can be clearly seen in this unique section, and when the line passes between the second and third piers at the eastern end of the Liskeard Viaduct, it is already almost 90ft below the level of Liskeard station. At 150ft, this was the second highest of Brunel's timber viaducts supported by masonry piers on the Cornwall main line, and it was rebuilt to its present form for single line working in 1894, being opened for normal double track operation on August 9th 1896. Having completed its curve, the connection again heads north to join the original L. & L. line at Coombe Junction (2 miles 5 chains) where there is still a single platform, with a small shelter and a signal box, although the runround loop, originally 476ft in length, has now been removed.

The L. & L. line continued northwards for a further 37 chains passing under a road bridge to reach Moorswater station, which was closed to passengers and replaced by Coombe Junction when the connecting line was brought into use on May 15th 1901, although the buildings were not completely demolished until almost fifty years later, in April or May 1951. An account written at the turn of the century described Moorswater station, which was to the east of the track, as having one platform about 20yds long, built of blocks of granite, with a sleeper border and covered with a layer of tarred granite chippings. The white painted wooden station building had a galvanised iron roof and was divided into two main sections, a booking office and

The original sheds at Moorswater in 1934

a waiting room, the amenities in the immediate area of the station being completed by a lavatory and a goods shed with a small metal canopy to provide shelter while transferring freight from rail to road. This station was in the very shadow of the Moorswater Viaduct, another of Brunel's timber structures, of which, although a completely new bridge was opened on February 25th 1881, the original masonry piers still stand, and indeed in November 1877 the Cornwall Railway had had to apply to the Canal Committee for permission to erect new piers at this point. There was a small signal box controlling a couple of sidings and two signal posts each with two arms controlling the ingoing and outgoing trains with double track in the station only and rails at this point laid on 2ft 6in square granite blocks. Indeed at this time there were three other types of permanent way besides approximately 2 miles mounted on stone blocks: modern bull-head rail had been used on the new connection, while stretchers of old flat bottom rail fastened directly to sleepers without chairs and sections of bridge rail on longitudinal sleepers were still to be found. In 1909 the following speed restrictions were in force: Looe to Coombe 20 mph; Liskeard to Coombe 10 mph; Caradon line 7 mph.

The Liskeard & Caradon headed northwards with sidings running off to the left to serve a Cornwall County Council Depot and a china clay drying plant whose traffic used to warrant one and sometimes two freights daily on Mondays to Fridays, although public freight facilities at Moorswater had been withdrawn since December 16th 1963. However the siding to the Cornwall County Council Depot has recently been closed and lifted, and at the time of writing the train only runs when required. Here, too, were the original shed and workshops of the Liskeard & Caradon Railway which were recorded in detail when the Great Western Railway took over the line in January 1909. There was a 40ft long locomotive shed with two roads each capable of holding an engine and coal wagon for bunkering as there was no coaling stage, although the shed possessed a small water tower. There was also a two road carriage repair shop 100ft in length while workshop facilities included a blacksmith's shop with a double hearth and a machine shop, with a 9in lathe, shaping machine, Whitworth pillar drilling machine, screwing machine and two small foot lathes. All these machines were driven by a water wheel six feet in diameter and with 4in treads, while the main equipment was completed by two sheer-legs, one inside and one outside. At this time Moorswater shed was used to stable the mineral engines for which only one set of men was necessary while two sets of men were needed to operate the passenger services whose engine was normally shedded at Looe. In later years the branch engines were all shedded at Moorswater shed until this was closed on September 11th 1961, when the branch passenger services were diesel-ised, and all the remaining buildings were demolished in 1969.

A siding to the right of the shed site is all that remains of the L. & C. main line which, although lifted for over fifty years, is still relatively easy to trace and its course is still shown on Ordnance Survey Maps. It passed under the main Truro Road and remained on a roughly parallel course until it reached Looe Mills before heading off northeastwards along the side of a wooded hill to begin its long climb to Caradon.

Passing through High Wood about three quarters of a mile from Looe Mills the line crossed a road on the level and at the time of writing the crossing gates are still in position although somewhat dilapidated. About half a mile further on it crossed another road on a bridge built of granite blocks, which was constructed to avoid the level crossing when the line was realigned to enable steam traction to be introduced. From here the railway continued on one of several very sharp horse-shoe bends to Treworgey where there was yet another level crossing whose gates still remain. Its course followed the road for a few hundred yards before disappearing into a cutting and under the main St. Cleer road at Tremabe Bridge where until 1957 there was a signpost bearing the inscription "To the Cheesewring Railway" but this has now been altered to read "St. Cleer". From this point much of the course of the line is indistinct as it curves around through rather desolate country to Tremar where it crossed the road on a bridge before reaching St. Cleer (4 miles 59 chains from Moorswater), the first sign of habitation. It crossed the road on the level, where traces of a relatively large layout still remain and the goods shed is still in use as a barn. Near here is one of the Cornish holy wells dedicated to St. Cleer or St. Clarus as he is often known.

From here the line curved through Trecarne and on to an embank-ment to reach Polwrath Siding, 1 mile 34 chains farther on, which served the mining village of Darite. Here there was a small stone goods shed while a finely built stone bridge carried the road over the line just south of the goods yard. There is still a road here running parallel with the course of the railway known as Railway Terrace and this was a regular stopping place for passengers in the heyday of the Caradon line. After Polwrath the line curved to the north to enter a shallow defile in the hills which after about a quarter of a mile opens out at the approach to Caradon (6 miles 33 chains from Moorswater and 13 miles 38 chains from Looe) to give a fascinating and somewhat eerie vista of the abandoned mine workings, the remains of whose shafts and engine houses are still visible surrounded by lumps of stone and grass grown mounds of spoil from the mines.

This was an important junction for the Caradon line, and a water tank was situated here for engines to replenish their supplies after the punishing climb from Moorswater. The main line ran to a dead end at the South Caradon mine while the older line to the Cheesewring went off steeply along the west side of Caradon Hill via Gonamena to reach Minions Mound and the quarries, and mineral tramways fanned out to serve the various mines in the immediate neighbourhood. A few stone block sleepers can still be found on this older route which, because of its gradients, was cable worked and, as can be imagined, provided an obstacle to speedy and efficient operation of the system. The three mile long newer line swept away eastward around the 1,213ft high Caradon Hill, but, because of the nature of the terrain, there was no direct connection from Moorswater and reversal was necessary at

Caradon mines in 1934 with the site of the original (Gonamena) line and stone sleepers in foreground

The new line on embankment between Crow's Nest and Tokenbury in 1934

this point near East Caradon Goods Siding. After a short stretch on a stone-faced embankment, the line continued on a moderate gradient across the moorland before heading northwards at Tokenbury Corner to follow the Liskeard–Launceston Road. At Tokenbury Siding, a small yard and sidings existed together with a goods shed to cater for the agricultural and mineral produce of the area. As the main road drops down to Upton the L. & C. line headed westward along the north side of Caradon Hill passing still more derelict mines including the Phoenix United Mine to which a branch headed off northwards, before rejoining the older line at Minions Mound where a small goods shed was situated just north of the road from Minions to Upton which the line through Gonamena had crossed on the level in the middle of the village. Close by this junction are the "Hurlers", those three stone circles which, according to legend, were the bodies of men turned to stone for going "hurling" on the Sabbath. The whole area around here is dotted with large boulders, the L. & C. having passed the celebrated cromlech known as the "Trethevy Stone", a huge table slab of granite balanced on six smaller upright blocks, during its climb towards Caradon. At this point the L. & C. was about 1,000ft above sea level although overshadowed by Caradon Hill, which was completely encircled by railways, but now, although its views over Dartmoor are unimpaired and the huge boulders cropping out of the earth are unchanged, its summit is graced by an I.T.A. television mast. From here it was but a short distance to the quarries, past the "Cheesewring" itself, an immense pile of blue grey granite with the smallest stone at the bottom and the largest, 34ft in diameter, precariously balanced on top. The line terminated at the quarries after running through somewhat desolate countryside and today it is indeed hard to believe that less than a century ago several thousand people lived and worked in this immediate area where now only the traces of ruined chimneys, engine houses and grass grown spoil heaps bear witness to the tragic end of the once prosperous Cornish mining industry, and together with the spoil heaps of the china clay mines are a memorable characteristic of the Cornish landscape. But besides the mineral traffic, the railway was also of great use to the rather scattered farming community and truck loads of fertilisers generally in the form of sand or seaweed were delivered along with coal to the various goods depots while wheat and other agricultural produce was also carried by rail to Liskeard and Looe.

North of here traces still remain of the line to the quarry near the 1,295ft Kilmar Tor on Twelve Men's Moor whose indented ridges are most impressive, and the abortive extension across Bodmin Moor which only reached Rushyford Gate on its way to Trewint Marsh. It is difficult today to appreciate the purpose or benefit of such an extension other than reaching the main Bodmin–Launceston road, although the further line projected until the 1884 Act would have taken it to a junction with the North Cornwall Railway. In this area, too, the landscape is dotted with boulders, tumuli and stone circles which add to the desolation and grandeur of the countryside.

Such then was the Liskeard & Caradon Railway, but the Liskeard & Looe line is still in use for passenger traffic, and passes through some most beautiful wooded scenery on its way to the sea. Heading south from Coombe, it runs back past the junction from which the line to Liskeard can be seen climbing steeply away. Between here and Looe the steepest gradient is only 1 in 121 and the line descends gently along the valley of the East Looe River with its tree- and bracken-covered hills dotted with whitewashed Cornish cottages and the occasional disused mine. The bridges are close to the coach sides as the line is single throughout and from time to time glimpses can be had of the abandoned canal which still contains water at some points, while two of the three public level crossings on the Looe line, Websters and Lodge Hill, are also to be found on this section.

The first station, St. Keyne (3 miles 64 chains from Liskeard), which first appeared in Bradshaw in October 1902, is a single platform graced by a small wooden shelter bearing a nameboard over its door. Near here is another Holy Well, this time dedicated to St. Keyne, a fifth century saint, and made famous by Southey's ballad, and canal, river and railway run side by side until the next station, Causeland (5 miles 9 chains) is reached. This was originally the only intermediate station on the line but it was closed for a period on the opening of Sandplace in December 1881 and did not reappear in the timetable until June 1888. It too has a small sleeper hut as a shelter, hidden among the trees with the clear stream running near, but no trace of human habitation so that one may perhaps wonder why it was ever built, although the hamlet of Trewidland is not far away to the north and some cottages are grouped around Landlooe Bridge.

Between here and Sandplace (6 miles 39 chains), opened in December 1881, the line passes through some of the most impressive scenery on the branch while bridges spanning river, railway and the canal with traces of disused locks all add charm to the journey. Sandplace in earlier days had some lime kilns which could be served from river or canal and where sand was collected from underwater banks by barges behind which were towed canvas bags held open by iron hoops. This was then loaded onto pack horses, whose pannier flaps could be opened to allow the sand to pour directly onto the fields where it was used as fertiliser. There are now a few cottages and a Post Office near the halt which, like the others, has a simple wooden hut on its platform, but it is not far from Morval, formerly the estate of Mr Buller, at whose request and that of Mr Edgcumbe in 1877–8 a siding was laid in from which passenger or mixed trains often collected wagons and propelled these to Looe while still hauling the original train. This practice, particularly when loading of timber was concerned, caused fouling of the running line and this finally had to be carried out only when hand signalmen were provided.

The line, which here is very prone to flooding, continues over the third public level crossing at Tarras and along the ever widening estuary of the East Looe River to reach Looe station (8 miles 51 chains) which is only a few feet from the water's edge close to the confluence of the East and West Looe Rivers. From this point there is a fine view across

The goods depot at Minions in 1934

Causeland Halt circa 1902

the broad estuary to the wooded hills beyond and southward to where the picturesque houses of the twin townships nestle on the slopes of the hills. East Looe appears more ancient and quaint with its narrow streets and Old Guildhall but traces of a Celtic settlement and monastery still survive on the hills above West Looe. This is one of the loveliest spots on the Cornish coast with a situation similar to Fowey and Falmouth where a narrow entrance from the open sea leads to a land-locked harbour from which an estuary penetrates inland for several miles. The river is spanned by a fine seven arch bridge opened in 1855 which replaced a 15th century structure some 100yds downstream. This had thirteen arches and there was on it a small chapel or oratory dedicated to St. Anne.

The branch has been successively cut back in recent years and the station buildings have recently been demolished and replaced by a bus-type shelter at the north end of the platform, much of the trackbed on from this point being used to provide car parking facilities. No run-round loop or sidings have been necessary with diesel multiple unit operation of passenger service since the withdrawal of freight services from the branch on November 4th 1963. These previously ran into a small goods yard in which there were run-round facilities for passenger trains, a goods shed, and a coal depot. A small single road corrugated iron engine shed 30ft in length was built at the turn of the century together with a 100ft single road carriage shed of the same material but both these closed sometime in the 1920's following complaints by local residents. From here a line ran past Looe Bridge alongside the main street before dividing into three and on to Buller Quay from which in the nineteenth century huge loads of granite blocks and mineral ore were loaded into sailing boats. Some of this line was laid on stone blocks but mainly on longitudinal wooden sleepers. During the last few years of its existence it merely provided facilities for local fish merchants and a boat building firm as since the Second World War the commercial importance of Looe as a port has been negligible. Traffic did not justify the continuation of these facilities so after being disused since about 1951 the quay sidings were officially closed on March 23rd 1954, after British Railways and the Looe Harbour Commissioners had decided to cover the track to avoid costly repairs and simplify the resurfacing of the car park. Nowadays, as mentioned above, the motor car has encroached on the site of the goods yard and even of the passenger station itself, and this has only barely escaped the threat of closure.

Although in the early days of the railway at Looe derailments were probably a reasonably frequent occurrence, little has been recorded about them as they were obviously considered a part of everyday life. After the opening of the connection to Liskeard, operation became a little more sophisticated but certain rather dangerous practices continued unabated, and one of these, the arrangements for delivery of coal to Looe Gas Works, is worth recounting in some detail. It was common practice for years to leave one or more loaded coal wagons on the main line after they had been uncoupled from the last train of the day. They would then be emptied and left on the main line to be propelled into Looe goods yard by the first train down the branch, ready for collection by the next freight train. This practice worked all right as long as the crews remembered the wagons on the main line and did not hurtle into them at full speed.

| Looe Bible Christian SUNDAY SCHOOL. JULY 26th, 1906. LOOE TO LISKEARD. Railway Ticket. This portion to be delivered to the Company on the UP Journey. | Looe Bible Christian SUNDAY SCHOOL. JULY 26th, 1906 LISKEARD TO LOOE. Railway Ticket. This portion to be delivered to the Company on the DOWN Journey. | LOOE BIBLE CHRISTIAN SUNDAY SCHOOL THURSDAY, JULY 26th, CHILDREN'S Excursion and Tea Ticket. This Portion to be given up at the Tea Tables. |

CHAPTER 8

Passenger Services

As we have seen, both the Caradon and Looe lines were originally envisaged purely for the transportation of minerals and other freight and no provision had been made to obtain sanction for passenger traffic. Yet, in their heyday some of the larger mines in the Caradon area employed over five hundred people and many of the others upwards of a hundred, so that the surface population in this once deserted moorland could be numbered in thousands. As the roads linking the area to Liskeard were anything but good, and public transport virtually non-existent, the inhabitants became most adept at getting lifts on the freight trains to and from Moorswater and at times right through to Looe. In the early days on the Caradon line the Directors had merely turned a blind eye to this practice but when they perceived the possibilities of obtaining extra revenue as well as providing a social service they introduced a system of providing free passes for intending passengers but collecting a small fee of 2d or 3d according to the distance travelled, ostensibly for carrying personal belongings such as hats, umbrellas and parcels. This practice was soon extended to the Looe line for it is recorded that on November 5th 1872, the Canal Committee discussed the possibility of issuing passes for journeys between Moorswater and Looe, which they finally agreed to do on April 8th of the following year, at the same time empowering Mr Trathan to issue passes for both the Looe and Caradon sections as required. These passengers were carried in open trucks at the rear of the mineral trains although a few lucky ones might gain refuge in the brake van in inclement weather. Indeed, as time went on, both companies even advertised places of interest on their lines to attract the passenger traffic they were not yet entitled to carry, although this practice only became really prevalent on the Caradon section after regular passenger services had commenced on the Looe line.

By the mid-seventies it was felt that the Moorswater–Looe section in particular could be exploited to carry a profitable passenger traffic and preparations were made for this eventuality. After certain improvements had been made to the track, application was made to the Board of Trade for the necessary sanction to operate passenger trains on this section, and on September 6th 1879, its Inspector, Colonel Rich, visited the line and carried out a rigorous inspection. He was obviously satisfied with what he had seen for a regular weekday service of two trains in each direction commenced on September 11th. Trains left Moorswater at 9.50 am and 4.30 pm and after a stop at Causeland reached Looe at 10.20 am and 5.00 pm respectively. The return workings left Looe at

10.50 am and 5.45 pm and were also allowed exactly half an hour for the journey with the one intermediate stop. An additional train leaving Moorswater at 6.45 pm and returning from Looe at 7.20 pm operated on Saturdays only. Single fares for the whole distance were 1s 6d first and 8d third class with returns at 2s 6d and 1s 2d respectively. There was a single fare to Causeland of 1s first and 4d third class but there appears to have been no return fare to and from this stop in the early days. In order to facilitate the transfer of passengers between Moorswater and the main line at Liskeard, in June 1880 the L. & C. approached the Cornwall Railway for its co-operation in operating a coach between these two stations, but this was refused and the main line company seemed determined to ignore the very existence of its lowly neighbour.

The Liskeard & Caradon Railway, however, was quick to see the potential of passenger traffic on the Looe line which by now it both leased and worked, and its Directors began to seriously consider a properly authorised service to Caradon and the Cheesewring. Moreover, as in the early eighties the idea of a connection from Moorswater to Liskeard was once again being seriously considered, it was suggested that trains from Looe should be divided at Coombe, one portion to climb up to the main line by whatever devious route should be finally constructed, and the other be taken on through the hills to Caradon. Preliminary estimates were that the journey from Looe to the Cheesewring would take approximately one hour, but these were obviously over-optimistic as excursion trains at this time were allowed well over an hour for journeys from the Caradon area just to Liskeard. In 1882 the L. & C. Directors approached the Board of Trade for permission to operate a passenger service over their own line, but this was refused because of the sharp curves and steep gradients on the Caradon line as well as the rather primitive facilities available. Nevertheless, undeterred by mere formalities, the Company continued its unsanctioned activities although in a slightly more sophisticated and expensive manner than before.

Passengers intending to travel on the Caradon line purchased a ticket either at Moorswater or from the guard on the train, covering the journey between Looe and Moorswater although they did not wish to travel on this section. They were then given a free pass to cover the Caradon section and if they had purchased a first class ticket were entitled to travel in a small van while the Third Class passengers had to travel in open wagons. In the earlier part of 1879, a paper pass on which the holder's name was written had been issued to intending passengers but this method proved too cumbersome for the large numbers involved so a standard card pass was substituted. This practice was such a part of everyday life that cheap rates were available for school or Sunday school parties, the headmaster or superintendent purchasing tickets from the guard after the heads had been ceremoniously counted. As many as forty truck loads of scholars and excursionists were taken up the line at certain times hauled by two or even all three locomotives. On return journeys, however, the locomotives

No. 4559 arriving at St. Keyne Halt with a passenger train from Liskeard in September 1958

followed the train back to Moorswater as this was split up in sections to be run down by gravity with a brakesman in charge of groups of four or five trucks each fitted with a small end footplate and screw brake. As there were several level crossings on the Caradon section this could be a somewhat hazardous undertaking although a man was stationed at each crossing to open the gates and the brakesmen and guards were provided with horns to warn the crossing keepers of their approach. Some idea of the scope and timings of such excursions can be seen from the following advertisement appearing in the "Cornish Times" for September 16th 1882:

EXCURSION TO LOOE
The last for the Season

On Monday, September 25th, a Train will run from Rillaton Bridge, Cheesewring, to Looe and back, leaving Rillaton Bridge 8.30 am, Tokenbury Corner 8.40; Railway Terrace 9.00; St. Cleer 9.10; Liskeard 9.52; returning from Looe at 5.30 pm. Tickets for the double journey 1s if purchased on or before Friday September 22nd, after this date 1s 3d. Children half-price. Proceeds to be devoted to reduction of debt on Minions Chapel U.M.F.C. Tickets may be obtained at Minions from Mr T. Hony; Sibly Back, Mr Higgins, Mr Albert Williams; Crow's Nest, Miss M. Dawe; Caradon Town, Mr Wm. Truscott; Ley Mill, Pensilva; Mr W. H. Drew; Mr J. Browning; St. Cleer, Mr Trigg; Chapel House; Railway Terrace, Mr Pascoe; Mr T. Moon, Fore Street.

As excursions from Moorswater to the Races at Looe, which was about half the distance, had return fares of 2s first class and 1s 3d third class the above excursion represented exceptional value although it must be remembered that the passengers from north of Moorswater would normally be travelling in open wagons, but no doubt getting covered in smuts from the engine and wet through in rainy weather was an integral part of the enjoyment particularly for the children of the miners and farmers on their great adventure to the seaside.

Even as late as 1885 when the mining district was in its death throes, it was felt worthwhile to advertise the existence of facilities for excursions north of Liskeard as in the "Cornish Times" of May 30th 1885, although this was merely given in a footnote:

Liskeard & Looe and Liskeard & Caradon Railways

On Wednesday, June 3rd, and following Wednesdays until further notice, Cheap Excursion Tickets will be issued from Moorswater to Looe by the Trains leaving Moorswater at 2.00 pm and 4.00 pm available to return by the trains leaving Looe at 7.00 pm and 8.25 pm. Tickets are not transferable.

N.B.   Special arrangements can be made with Friendly Societies, School etc., for Excursion Trains to Looe or Cheesewring on application to:

J. Smythurst,
Traffic Superintendent.

The closure of the mines and the virtual depopulation of the Caradon area brought to an end the large scale carrying of passengers north of Moorswater in 1886, which was perhaps just as well as the condition of the track was allowed to deteriorate and the risk of derailments and serious accidents became consequently greater. About 1896 the practice of carrying passengers on the Caradon section was officially abandoned but no doubt any remaining inhabitants of the area continued their old habits, getting a ride at the Company's expense and leaping on and off just outside the confines of Moorswater station. Nevertheless in the heyday of the mines the practice of charging for passengers' baggage and issuing free passes had most certainly been carried on in an official manner to specific rules as witnessed by an L. & C. notice still standing at Tokenbury in 1909 and reported in the G.W.R. Magazine for February of that year:

"FREE PASSES. CONDITIONS ON WHICH ALONE PERSONS ARE PERMITTED TO TRAVEL BY THE TRAINS ON THIS RAILWAY.

No persons to travel on the trains without a pass. All passes are issued gratuitously, but solely on the conditions that they are to be used only by the person in whose favour they are issued, and that the use of any free pass, or the fact of travelling gratuitously over any of the railway of the Company, shall be taken as evidence of an agreement with the Directors that neither the Company nor the Directors or their servants are to be responsible for any injury or damage which may occur to any person travelling by a free pass through accident, delay or otherwise, whether occasioned by any act or neglect of the Company or its servants or otherwise, or for loss or damage to property, however caused.

All passes are only available on the day for which issued; they must be exhibited when required and be given up at the end of the journey, and the holder is subject to the Byelaws and other general regulations of the Company.

By Order of the Directors,
Liskeard & Caradon Railway."

After the closure of the mines, passenger services on the Looe section became of prime importance for the continuing survival of the two companies. Over 21,000 passengers a year were being carried by 1883, 22,767 were carried in 1885 and 25,429 in the following year, the number of tickets issued being as follows: 1st Class: 315; 2nd Class: 7,115; 3rd Class: 4,154; Excursion tickets, which were issued on certain days at 1s od return: 13,845. The August 1887 Bradshaw shows three trains in each direction on weekdays, of which the morning working each way was first and second class only. The price of first class singles had remained at 1s 6d while second class singles were 9d with third class singles reduced by 1d to 7d.

As mentioned above, the L. & C. had approached the Cornwall Railway with a scheme to share the costs of a coach between Moorswater and Liskeard but this had been turned down. Indeed, although the Cornwall main line passed over the Looe line at Moorswater only about ¾ mile by road from Liskeard station and the L. & L. had even provided a special exchange platform at Coombe, neither the C.R., nor after its amalgamation with the G.W.R. on July 1st 1889, the major company, made any mention of this in their timetables but advertised instead road vehicles running between Menheniot station and Looe. Known locally as "Martins Bus", two conveyances ran daily from Looe. One left at 8 am and remained all day at Menheniot while the 11 am wagonette returned to Looe almost at once, after arriving at the main line station. An account by a traveller at the turn of the century would seem to indicate that the local company had a kind of vicarious revenge for this snub as the stations at Looe and Moorswater both exhibited Caledonian Railway timetables and on the opening of the connection to the G.W.R. main line at Liskeard, "Martins Bus" ceased to run.

Even at this date the intermediate stations were unstaffed and tickets were issued by the guards on the trains. A brief mention of the tickets used by the Looe Company is perhaps appropriate here. As far as singles were concerned, 1st class tickets were white, but for journeys from Moorswater to Looe 2nd class tickets were rose pink while in the opposite direction buff tickets were issued. The same distinction applied to 3rd class tickets, blue being used for the up direction and green for trains to Moorswater. Most return tickets were bi-coloured but there were obviously some variations in this scheme from time to time.

It is interesting to note that even in 1896 when the mining industry was all but finished in the area, that out of total receipts of £2,210 11s 9d no less than £1,522 18s 8d had come from freight traffic and indeed the total number of passengers carried had fallen slightly in the previous ten years being 23,980, while in 1897 a further slight decline to 23,654 took place.

Comparison between the number of passengers carried in 1886 and 1897 shows some interesting trends in the travelling habits of those using the line particularly the decline in second class passengers and the immense growth in the number of third class tickets issued:

Year	1st	2nd	3rd	Excursion	Total
1886	315	7,115	4,154	13,845	25,429
1897	142	854	15,775	6,883	23,654

This decline in the number of passengers carried continued in the next few years and no improvements were made in the train service so that in March 1901 there were still only two trains per day leaving Moorswater at 9.50 am and 3.30 pm and returning from Looe at 11.00 am and 5.00 pm respectively. The journey time was still 30 minutes in each direction, but there were now intermediate stops at Sandplace and Causeland, while for the exchange platform at Coombe it was stated "the trains will stop at Coombe for passengers booking to Moorswater and going to the G.W. Station at Liskeard, notice to be given to the guard at Looe."

After the opening of the new connection to the G.W. main line in May 1901, there was a great upsurge in passenger traffic and on Whit Monday no less than seven trains each way were operated between Looe and Liskeard. This was followed by a basic weekday service of four trains in each direction but on Monday, August 19th 1901, the L. & L. Directors, who were now responsible for operating both their own line and the Caradon section, decided to suspend the late night trains operated on Wednesdays and Saturdays for the months of November to April inclusive. Moreover it was also agreed that the 7.40 pm departure from Liskeard should be discontinued and replaced by a train leaving at 7.05 pm. A timetable for the period January to April 1902 gave departures from Looe at 8.35 am, 12.10 pm, 3.50 pm and 6.05 pm returning from Liskeard at 10.25 am, 2.20 pm, 4.55 pm and 7.05 pm. The time for the 8¾ mile journey was 35 minutes which included stops at Sandplace and Causeland and the stop and reversal at Coombe Junction. For Looe Regatta on August Bank Holiday Monday, 1907, a special service of twelve trains each way was programmed, the last train leaving Looe at 10.45 pm. In the summer of 1908, the last year of independent operation, there was a basic weekday service of seven trains from Liskeard to Looe and six in the opposite direction with an additional up train on three days and an extra down train on four days of the week.

10.10 am D.M.U. from Looe at Sandplace Halt in September 1966

Passenger traffic had certainly increased immensely not merely because of improved facilities and additional trains but also because of the zeal of the Traffic Manager, Mr Holbrook, who made sure his railway was kept before the public not merely by straightforward advertising but also by detailed and accurate reporting of its activities in the local press. In 1900, the last year before the connection to the G.W. was opened, only 21,000 people had been carried on the line while in 1908 no less than 70,798 passengers travelled, a more than threefold increase. The Directors and, of course, Mr Holbrook made a point of listening to their customers' complaints and suggestions and were quick to act on any thing which might rebound to their advantage so that in its last years the L. & L. was a most friendly and well run line where travellers were made welcome to the very limit of the company's resources.

Even at this late stage a rail motor service up the Caradon line was seriously suggested as it was stated that the population between Liskeard and Caradon was greater than that between Liskeard and Looe, but nothing ever came of this. Under the aegis of the G.W. some of this family feeling engendered by the Looe Railway was unavoidably lost but improvements were nonetheless made in the services and by April 1910 a Sunday service of two trains from Liskeard to Looe was in operation although there was only one train in the opposite direction, while on weekdays seven trains operated to Looe and six to Liskeard, with an extra train in each direction on Saturdays only and an extra Monday morning train back to Liskeard to balance the Sunday working. However, it was soon felt that this was perhaps excessive and by October 1914 there were only five trains in each direction on weekdays with two extra on Saturdays, as well as an additional up train on Mondays only, while on Sundays there were two down trains and one up, the balancing working being the extra Monday train. The journey time had now been reduced to 30 minutes even though there had been an additional stop since October 1902 at St. Keyne. A mixed train ran from Liskeard at 5.30 am every day including Sundays and although it did not stop at Causeland it was allowed 32 minutes for the journey to Looe. The service was only slightly increased over the years and by July 1938, a basic service of eight trains each way operated on Mondays to Fridays, with the same number of trains on Sundays. Summer Saturday services were more complex with seven basic trains in each direction and six extra services between Liskeard and Looe of which two ran non-stop apart from reversal at Coombe, but there were only three additional workings in the opposite direction.

After the Second World War the basic pattern differed little, although numbers of extra trains ran on summer Saturdays, and to take the 1954 winter service as a representative sample, there were nine trains on weekdays in each direction with an extra working Saturdays. In summer an additional late trip was run on Fridays and on Saturdays there were twelve return workings including the early morning trips which did not call at intermediate stations. There was also a summer Sunday service of 6 trains each way. Usually at this time passenger trains consisted of two or three non-corridor coaches, the 7.15 am from Liskeard to Looe being regarded as a mixed train as it sometimes hauled one or two wagons. On dieselisation of the passenger services at the start of the 1961 winter timetable, eight weekday trains were provided in each direction with an extra late night working on Saturdays. The weekday service was increased to nine in the summer of 1965 while the summer Saturday trains in the mid sixties averaged between ten and eleven in each direction, with a Sunday service of between five and seven trains operating during the summer months only. Traffic, although relatively heavy in summer, is very light in winter when a single unit is sufficient in place of the two or three car set usual for summer weekend operation. Small wonder then that withdrawal of the Liskeard–Looe passenger services and complete closure of the Coombe Junction–Looe section was proposed for October 4th 1965. All freight was by that time already being carried by road apart from china clay traffic at Moorswater and the branch signal box at Liskeard had been closed and its instruments transferred to the main line box while the whole line was controlled by the stationmaster at Liskeard. The single line between Liskeard and Looe, with Coombe as the only intermediate crossing point, had been worked by electric train token until the withdrawal of freight trains to Looe from November 4th 1963, since when "one engine in steam" working has applied south of Coombe, the few chains north of Coombe to Moorswater being worked as a long siding using a wooden staff. The seven lever signalbox at Looe was closed on March 3rd 1964, as there was no longer any use for it. The token instrument was kept in the booking office there while the locking frames at Liskeard Branch and Coombe Junction were of Saxby & Farmer manufacture, a type probably unique on the G.W.R. and a relic of the independent Liskeard & Looe Railway.

As the intermediate stations had always been unstaffed halts, further large scale operating economies were difficult to envisage, and after the usual objections had been heard, withdrawal of passenger services was scheduled for October 5th 1966. Indeed in common with several other West Country services, summer Sunday trains were not listed in the 1966 timetable although these did in fact run. Nevertheless, passenger services were ultimately reprieved by the Minister of Transport because of the difficulty of providing substitute bus services, particularly during the peak summer holiday season.

Since then further economies have in fact been made for ticket issuing facilities were withdrawn from Looe and the station was completely destaffed from Monday, September 30th 1968. From May 19th 1969, in conjunction with the rest of the stations between Liskeard and Plymouth, ticket issuing facilities were withdrawn from the former, thus placing all fare collection for the branch in the hands of conductor guards armed with Omniprinter machines. Nevertheless the branch still required four men to operate it, the driver and guard on the train, the signalman at Coombe and a crossing keeper at Tarras Bridge, the only main road crossing on the line, but this was destaffed in 1970 and the crossing gates removed.

On November 15th 1968, the Minister of Transport announced the first list of passenger services to be grant-aided and the Liskeard–Looe line was included in this although it was not until January 28th 1969, that the actual amount of £36,000 for one year was announced. Since then this has been renewed at an annual figure of £35,000 for 1970 and 1971, followed by a two-year grant of £60,000 for 1972-3. For 1974 all Cornwall's railways are receiving a total of £925,000. In view of the government's recent pronouncements on the future of railways the Looe branch seems certain to remain open even after much-needed road improvements have taken place. A service of nine trains each way on weekdays continues to operate all the year round although times are slightly amended on Summer Saturdays while the Summer Sunday service of six trains in each direction also continues to run and it is reasonable to expect this pattern to continue in the foreseeable future.

APPENDIX

Article in Western Morning News, March 3rd, 1967
When "Kilmar" ran to Cheesewring—by R. V. Walling

Built in 1869, the *Kilmar* had no cab for its driver and fireman despite the climate in which it worked. There was just a flat, vertical weather-board with two "portholes" in it. On wet days the footplate men rigged a tarred canvas from it to the back of the coal bunker in order to obtain some shelter.

Every weekday morning the *Kilmar* would chuff its way from Moorswater Junction with a train of small trucks, one of them loaded with coal for the Cheesewring quarries.

There was a halt at the level crossing just below St. Cleer's Well unless some kind person happened to be passing and opened the gates. During school holidays there were lots of juvenile volunteers for the advent of the train was quite an event in their placid lives.

The same thing happened at the top of Tremar Coombe, near the little hollow in which was a spring of drinking water which we had to trundle home in barrels loaded onto wheelbarrows to the village that has now reverted to its ancient name, Darite.

Sixty years ago we called it Railway Terrace. Here was a siding little used it is true, but lending the place a sort of status. The train usually stopped and Mr Stephens, the guard, who had his name painted on the side of his van, would boil a kettle, with smoke pouring from the little chimney in the room, and "brew up" for all hands.

Then *Kilmar* would forge ahead, around the side of the steep hill above Crowsnest and up to the fabulous ruins of the Caradon mines that once made millions for investors, but looked like the views of Pompeii in our picture books.

The mouth of this grim Gonamena valley was too narrow for the railway to curve around to its eastern side. The line passed over points and came to a dead end. Mr Stephens got out, and shifted the points. The old engine then went hard astern and pushed its train up the gradient of Caradon's southern shoulder. It would then vanish beyond our ken into the remote land where lay mysterious places called Linkinhorne and Upton Cross and Minions.

Later in the day a train of trucks, loaded with huge blocks of granite and headed by Mr Stephens in his brake van, would come rumbling down the hill with a clack of wheels over rail joints and banging of hard, wooden buffers (the trucks had no spring buffers) over the junction and halt with squealing brakes.

The *Kilmar* would follow, hissing and sizzling and clanking, and be eased onto the other end of the train, the points would be altered and the train would be off on its way back to Moorswater.

On one memorable occasion it failed to make its destination. The approach to the crossing at Tremar Coombe was on an embankment. We had had some heavy downpours of rain. When the laden trucks were just short of the road, and the engine safely over, the big blocks of stone to which the rails were fastened moved outwards because there were no cross-ties and three or four trucks went down between them. What a shemozzle it was.

Next day *Kilmar* returned with a gang of men, big jacks and other tackle. The trucks were heaved up, the granite blocks were levered back, and the rails were spiked down again. It was no mean feat, really, without the aid of a crane, as the embankment was only just wide enough to take the track.

The old Caradon railway was already in decline in those days for none of the mines was working and stone from the quarries was the only freight. Then the stalwart old *Kilmar* packed up; the little *Lady Margaret* which had drawn the passenger trains from Liskeard to Looe, was demoted to the lowly Cheesewring route and her place taken by a bigger engine hired from the G.W.R., No. 13 I remember.

When, after being away from East Cornwall for three or four years, I went back for a holiday, I found the whole thing had been taken over by the Great Western and the track relaid with wooden sleepers and new rails.

Local people were talking about a passenger service. Alas, not only was that quite out of reckoning, but the goods trains were soon to be withdrawn. At the end of 1916, that beautiful new track was taken up, requisitioned by the War Department and taken across to Flanders to help replace the worn-out rails of the Chemin de Fer du Nord, which, during the Great War, probably carried the heaviest traffic ever known to railway operators.

It is interesting to note that when the Caradon line was converted from horse to steam traction—probably when the *Kilmar* was purchased—the route was altered slightly to ease one or two gradients.

Between Railway Terrace and the Caradon junction the old track could still be followed. Everyone walked along the railway for it was the nearest and easiest route between some places.

Several bridges remain today, a couple of them carrying the road over the old track. This, although much overgrown, can still be followed. How different it all is from those unhurried days when news of the mishap at Tremar had to be taken to Moorswater by a man on a bicycle because there was no telephone within miles.

From the 'Cornish Times' May 1901

"The Mishap"

"The Looe is off the line again"
Said one as he towards me came;
This was late last Wednesday night,
As I was going home, not tight.

Then for the station I went straight,
And though 'twas 'leven o'clock at night;
I found its lamps were burning bright,
And several people met my sight.

All waiting for their friends to come
To know what damage had been done
To them or any in the train,
All in suspense that's worse than pain.

Some had been there since ten o'clock
And most of them had their steam up
And all for want of sleep to dream
By twelve o'clock were wasting steam.

One lady said " 'Tis very hard,
My daughter cannot leave Liskeard;
How many passengers at Coombe
Have up to date there met some doom?"

"Upon this line to trouble prone,
You'll never know when you'll get home,
and Parliament must interfere
When is Sir Lewis coming here?"

Then spoke some gent "Upon the grass
The ill-used steed the night must pass
You're surer riding in a cart,
Behind a donkey when it's dark".

Some trains run late, some early through,
This one ran late and early too,
Officials tell the Cornishman
" 'Tis worked on the Great Eastern Plan".

Last Tuesday night another fright
Was witnessed on the line
The Caradon would not steam at all
For want of Adam's wine.

Bad luck there should be none left
For her to take her fill
And there to stick upon the rails
Against the driver's will.

One railman said "If there's no wine
Instead give her some beer:
Boss Peace he keeps a good supply
And lives just handy near".

And then for once they did agree
Each took a pail or tub,
And ran as fast as he could go
Into the little pub.

And there the taps were turned on full
For each to take his pail
And take it to the thirsty steed
That rested on the rail.

I do not know how much of beer
The Boss sold through that fright
But this I know, the best of beer
The Caradon drank that night.

Resident,
Fast Looe, May 27th 1901.

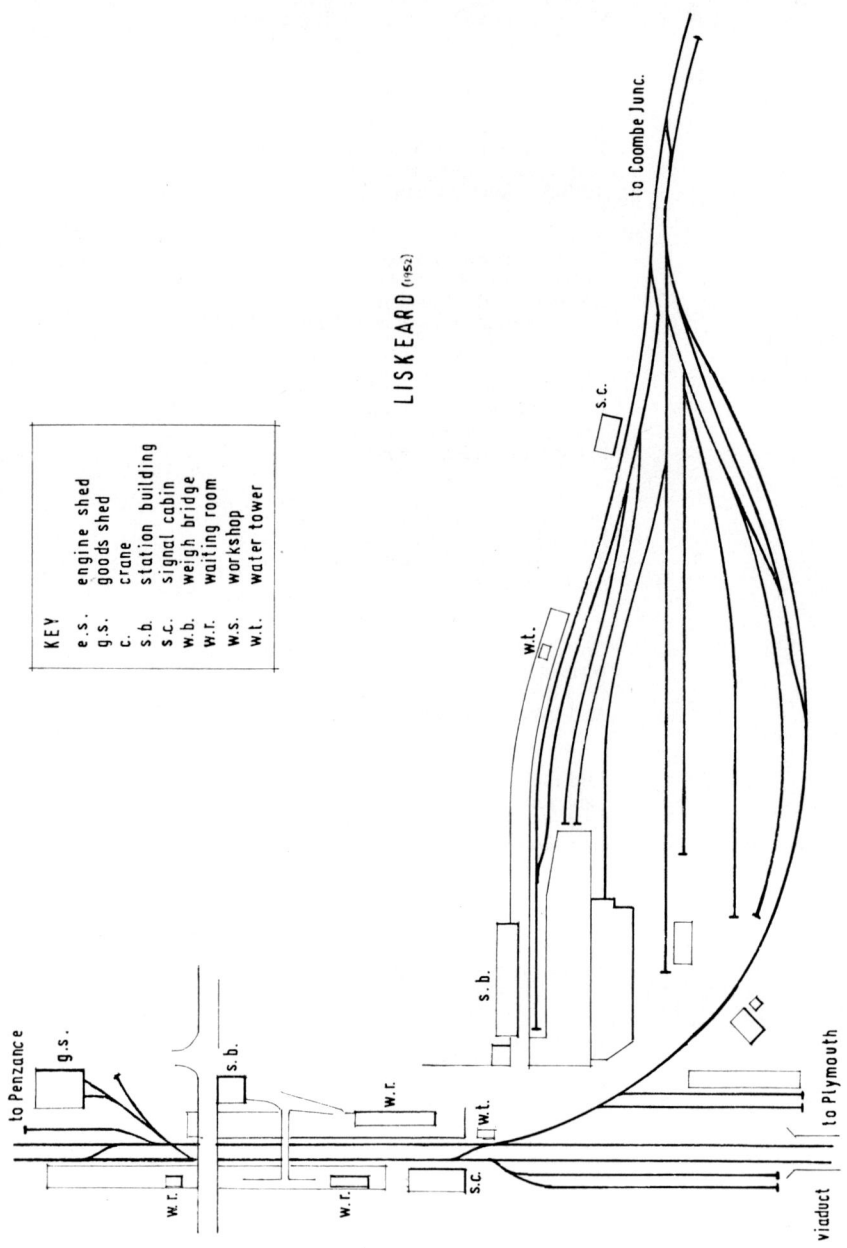

LISKEARD (1952)

KEY

e.s.	engine shed
g.s.	goods shed
c.	crane
s.b.	station building
s.c.	signal cabin
w.b.	weigh bridge
w.r.	waiting room
w.s.	workshop
w.t.	water tower

to Coombe Junc.

s.c.

w.t.

s.b.

to Penzance

g.s.

s.b.

w.r.

w.r.

w.r.

w.t.

s.c.

to Plymouth

viaduct

82

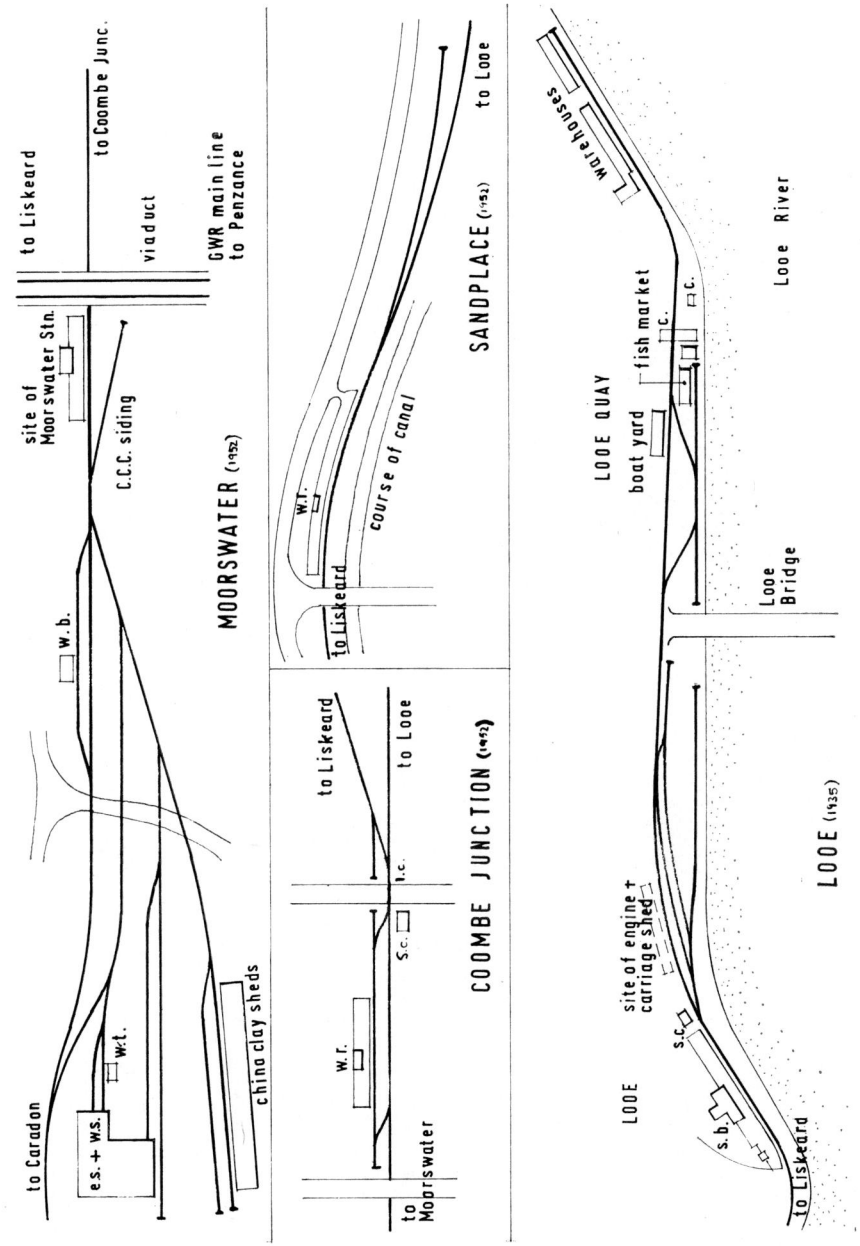

to Liskeard

to Coombe Junc.

site of
Moorswater Stn.

viaduct

GWR main line
to Penzance

C.C.C. siding

w.b.

to Caradon

w.t.

e.s. + w.s.

china clay sheds

MOORSWATER (1952)

course of canal

w.t.

to Liskeard

SANDPLACE (1952)

to Looe

to Liskeard

to Looe

l.c.

s.c.

w.r.

to
Moorswater

COOMBE JUNCTION (1952)

warehouses

LOOE QUAY

boat yard

fish market

l.c.

l.c.

Looe
Bridge

Looe River

LOOE

site of engine +
carriage shed

s.c.

s.b.

to Liskeard

LOOE (1935)

83

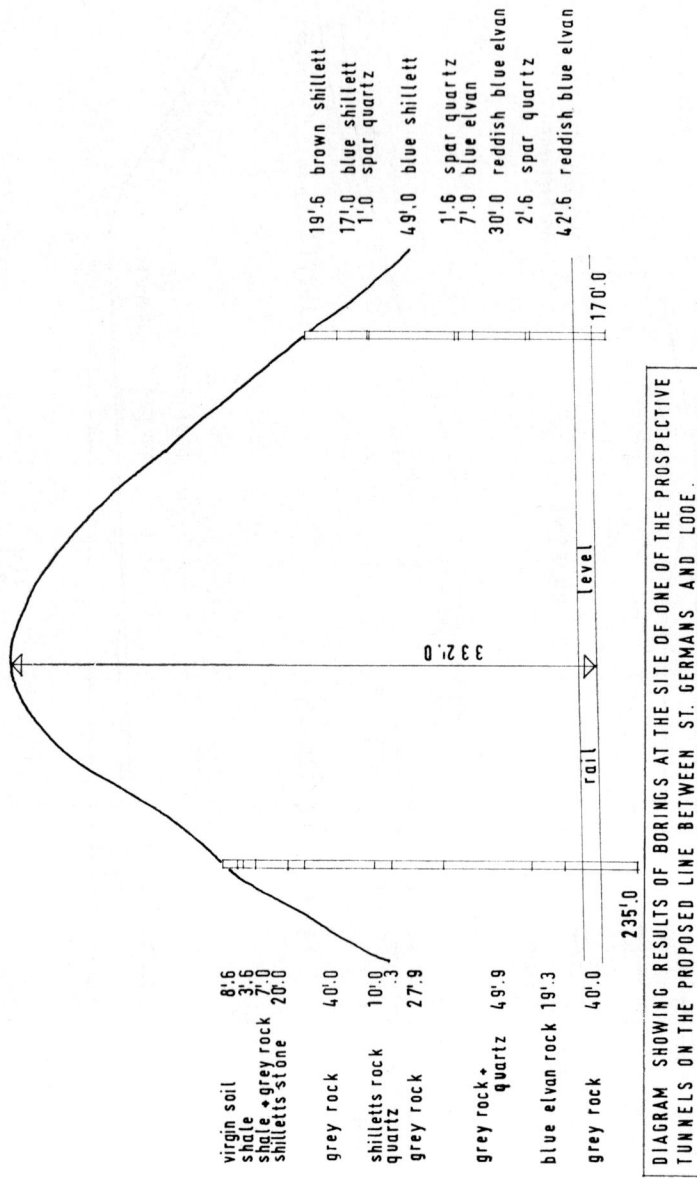

DIAGRAM SHOWING RESULTS OF BORINGS AT THE SITE OF ONE OF THE PROSPECTIVE
TUNNELS ON THE PROPOSED LINE BETWEEN ST. GERMANS AND LOOE.

SEPTEMBER 1879—Passenger trains, Weekdays only

					SO
MOORSWATER	dep.	9.50	4.30		6.45
Causeland		10.05	4.45		7.00
LOOE	arr.	10.20	5.00		7.15

				SO
LOOE	dep.	10.50	5.45	7.20
Causeland		11.05	6.00	7.35
MOORSWATER	arr.	11.20	6.15	7.50

SO   Saturdays only.

Fares: Looe to Moorswater or vice versa
1st class 1/6d single, 2/6d return
3rd class 8d single, 1/2d return

Looe or Moorswater to Causeland
1st class 1/-, 3rd 4d (returns not issued)

JANUARY TO APRIL 1902—Passenger trains, Weekdays only

LISKEARD	dep.	10.25	2.20	4.55	7.05
Coombe		10.35	2.30	5.05	7.15
Causeland		10.46	2.41	5.16	7.26
Sandplace		10.52	2.47	5.22	7.32
LOOE	arr.	11.00	2.55	5.30	7.40

LOOE	dep.	8.35	12.10	3.50	6.05
Sandplace		8.43	12.18	3.58	6.13
Causeland		8.49	12.24	4.04	6.19
Coombe		9.00	12.35	4.15	6.30
LISKEARD	arr.	9.10	12.45	4.25	6.40

MAY 1911

CARADON BRANCH

Blue triangular wooden train staff Coombe Junction to Moorswater
Oak colour round wooden train staff Moorswater to Rillaton Bridge

		Goods RR CS	Goods RR	Goods
COOMBE JUNCTION	dep.	7.35	8.20	10.13
Moorswater	arr.			10.18
Moorswater	dep.	7.08 (MX) from Looe	8.25 (8.05 from Liskeard)	10.45*
Polwrath Siding				CR
South Caradon				CR
Tokenbury Siding				CR
Rillaton Bridge				CR
Phoenix Siding				CR
Minions				
CHEESEWRING SIDING	arr.			

		Empty Cattle Trucks To Looe. Runs last Mon. in month	Goods RR To Liskeard	LE To Liskeard	To Looe last Mon. in month
CHEESEWRING SIDING	dep.	2.00*			
Minions		CR			
Phoenix Siding		CR			
Rillaton Bridge		CR			
Tokenbury Siding		CR			
South Caradon		CR			
Polwrath Siding		CR			
Moorswater	arr.	3.30			
Moorswater	dep.		8.15	5‖05	2.10
COOMBE JUNCTION	arr.	1.30	8/20	5‖08	2.13

CS   Calls only to exchange tablet or staff.   CR   Calls if required.   RR   Runs when required.
*   Will run as far as required and call where required. Will not run beyond Moorswater on Tuesdays and Thursdays unless specially wanted.

MAY 1911

		Exc'n Sats 22 Jly to 26 Aug	Exc'n SO	Mixed	Exc'n Sats 10/17/ 24 Jun, 1 Jly	Goods RR		Goods
LISKEARD	dep.	3.30	5.46	5.30	7.20	8.05	9.15	10.00	10.55
Stop Board						P		P	
Coombe Junc.	arr.	3.42	5.58	5.37	7.27	8.18	9.22		11.02
	dep.	3.45	6.07	5.42	7.34	8x20	9.25	10/13	11.05
St. Keyne				5.47	7.39	M	9.30	M	11.10
Causeland		SUSPENDED			7.43		9.34		11.14
Sandplace				5.56	7.48		9.39		11.19
LOOE	arr.	4.00	6.27	6.02	7.54		9.45		11.25

		ECS Sats 22 Jly to 26 Aug	ECS SO	LE	ECS Sats 10/17/ 24 Jun, 1 Jly	MO	Goods MX	Goods RR	Goods §RR
LOOE	dep.	2†43	4†55		6†40	6.45	7.08		
Sandplace						6.51	CR		M
Causeland		SUSPENDED				6.56	CR		
St. Keyne						7.00	CR		
Coombe Junc.	arr.	3.00	5.15	M	6.59	7.04			
	dep.	3.10	5.19	5‖13	7.02	7.07	CS	7.35	8x20
LISKEARD	arr.	3†18	5†27	5‖22	7†10	7.15	M	7.47	8.32

Sundays

			LE		
LOOE	dep.	4‖50	10.20	6.45
Sandplace			10.26	6.51
Causeland			10.31	6.56
St. Keyne			10.35	7.00
Coombe Junc.	arr.	5.08	10.39	7.04
	dep.	5.10	10.42	7.07
LISKEARD	arr.	5‖18	10.50	7.15

NOTES:

CR	Calls when required	RR	Runs only when required
CS	Calls only to exchange tablets	SO	Saturdays only
ECS and †	Empty Coaching Stock	WThSO	Wednesdays, Thursdays and
L	Runs when required on last		Saturdays only
	Monday in month only	*	Light engine to Moorswater as
LE and ‖	Light Engine		soon as possible
M	To or from Moorswater	§	When run a portion of 7.08 Looe
MO	Mondays only		is placed in the siding at Coombe
MX	Mondays excepted		Junc. Train returns from Lis-
P	Stops to pin down brakes		keard at 8.05 and takes remaining
			traffic to Moorswater

Empty Cattle Trucks L		WThSO				WThSO	**Sundays** Mixed		
1.15		2.40	4.55	7.30	9.40		5.30	11.05	9.00
	M								
1.22	2.13	2.47	5.02	7.37	9.47		5.37	11.12	9.07
1.25	2.15	2.50	5.05	7.40	9.50		5.40	11.15	9.10
1.30		2.55	5.10	7.45	9.55		5.45	11.20	9.15
1.34		2.59	5.14	7.04	9.59			11.24	9.19
1.39		3.04	5.19	7.54	10.04		5.54	11.29	9.24
1.45	2.30	3.10	5.25	8.00	10.10		6.00	11.35	9.30

			WThSO		Cattle L		WThSO
8.25	10.00	12.15	2.00	3.55	5.35	6.40	8.30
8.31	10.06	12.21	2.06	4.01		6.46	8.36
8.36	10.11	12.26	2.11	4.06		6.51	8.41
8.40	10.15	12.30	2.15	4.10		6.55	8.45
8.44	10.19	12.34	2.19	4.14	5.56	6.59	8.49
8.47	10.22	12.37	2.22	4.17	6.00	7.02	8.52
8.55	10.30	12.45	2.30	4.25	6.10*	7.10	9.00

14th June to 19th September 1954

LISKEARD		SO Z	SO	Mixed N	SO M	SO	SX	SX V	SO
LISKEARD	dep.	4‡43	5‡58	7.15 P	8†00	8.41	8.55	9.55	10.03
Stop Board									
Coombe Junc.	arr.				8.07			10.02	
	dep.	CS	CS	7.25	8x14	8.51	9.05	10x07	10x17
St. Keyne Halt				7.30		8.56	9.10	10.12	10.22
Causeland Halt		++ 4.40	++ 5.55	7.34		9.00	9.14	10.16	10.26
Sandplace Halt				7.38		9.04	9.18	10.20	10.30
LOOE	arr.	5.10	6.25	7.44	8†31	9.10	9.24	10.26	10.36

LOOE		SO	SO	SO	SX	SO	L	SO	SX
LOOE	dep.	5†20	6.35	7.52	8.10	9.25	9.45	10.45	11.15
Sandplace Halt				7.58	8.16		9.51	10.51	11.21
Causeland Halt				8.02	8.20		9.55	10.55	11.25
St. Keyne Halt				8.06	8.24		9.59	10.59	11.29
Coombe Junc.	arr.					9.43	10.06		
	dep.	CS	CS	8x15	8.33	9x46	10x09	11.08	11.38
LISKEARD	arr.	5†48	7.03	8.23	8.41	9.56	10.17	11.16	11.46

Sundays

LISKEARD		VV					
LISKEARD	dep.	9.00	10.45	12.15	1.55	4.31	7.41
Stop Board							
Coombe Junc.	arr.						
	dep.	9.10	10.55	12.25	2.05	4.41	7.51
St. Keyne Halt		9.15	11.00	12.30	2.10	4.46	7.56
Causeland Halt		9.19	11.04	12.34	2.14	4.50	8.00
Sandplace Halt		9.23	11.08	12.38	2.18	4.54	8.04
LOOE	arr.	9.29	11.14	12.44	2.24	5.00	8.10

Notes:

A	Moorswater arr. 12.27, dep. 1.00 for Coombe Junction
CS	Calls only to exchange tokens
FSO	Fridays and Saturdays only
H	May be held until 11.52 for 11.35 pm (FO) Liverpool-Penzance (or 10.45 am North Road if preceding)
K	Runs 15 minutes later on Saturdays
L	Runs 10 minutes later on Saturdays
M	Light engine ex Moorswater 7.35. May run as a passenger train if required
N	Light engine ex Moorswater 6.15 SX. Must run punctually SO
P	Stops to pin down brakes
Q	Runs 5 minutes later on Saturdays
SO	Saturdays only

SO H	SX	Goods		SO	SX	Q	Q		FSO U
11.25	11‡57	12.10	1.24	2‡54	3.05	4.35	5.50	7.45	9.13
	++ 11.55	P 12A23		++ 2.52					
11.35	12.07	1A04	1.34	3.04	3.15	4.45	6.00	7.55	9.23
11.40	12.12		1.39	3.09	3.20	4.50	6.05	8.00	9.28
11.44	12.16		1.43	3.13	3.24	4.54	6.09	8.04	9.32
11.48	12.20		1.47	3.17	3.28	4.58	6.13	8.08	9.36
11.54	12.26	1.28	1.53	3.23	3.34	5.04	6.19	8.14	9.44

SO	SX		Goods	Q	K			FSO U
12.30	12.40	2.10	2.42	3.50	5.12	6.30	8.30	9.50
12.36	12.46	2.16		3.56	5.18	6.36	8.36	9.56
12.40	12.50	2.20		4.00	5.22	6.40	8.40	10.00
12.44	12.54	2.24		4.04	5.26	6.44	8.44	10.04
			¶				8.50	
12.53	1.03	2.33	3.20	4.13	5.35	6.53	8.53	10.12
1.01	1.11	2.41	3.31	4.21	5.43	7.01	9.01Y	10.20YY

Sundays

LOOE	dep.	9.55	11.24	1.10	2.50	6.30	8.20
Sandplace Halt		10.01	11.30	1.16	2.56	6.36	8.26
Causeland Halt		10.05	11.34	1.20	3.00	6.40	8.30
St. Keyne Halt		10.09	11.38	1.24	3.04	6.44	8.34
Coombe Junc. arr.		10.00					
	dep.	10.18	11.47	1.33	3.13	6.53	8.43
LISKEARD	arr.	10.26	11.55	1.41	3.21	7.01	8.51ZZ

SX	Saturdays excepted
U	Also runs Monday 2nd August
V	Light engine ex Moorswater 9.30
VV	Light engine ex Moorswater 8.40
Y	Light engine to Moorswater 9.05 except when 9.13 Liskeard running
YY	Light engine to Moorswater 10.25
Z	Light engine ex Moorswater 4.20
ZZ	Light engine to Moorswater 9.00
‡	Advertised time
†	Empty coaching stock
¶	Coombe Junction 3/2, Moorswater arr. 3.04 dep. 3.17

Other titles from Forge Books . . .

ADVENTURERS' SLOPES
by DOUGLAS STUCKEY

The story of the silver and other mines of
Combe Martin in Devon. $22\frac{1}{2}$p

DAYS OF RENOWN by J. M. SLADER

The mines of Exmoor and the border parishes. $47\frac{1}{2}$p

MEN AND MINING ON THE QUAN-TOCKS by J. F. LAWRENCE and JOHN HAMILTON

The first account of the Nether Stowey mines
with a rich background of social history.   75p

Available from booksellers or direct from

FORGE BOOKS

42 Rectory Lane - Bracknell - Berkshire

Printed by Lonsdale Universal Printing Ltd., Bath